NUMEROLOGY

Your Destiny Decoded: Personal Numerology For Beginners

Serra Night

Table of Contents

Introduction 1

Chapter 1: What is Numerology? 3

Chapter 2: The Philosophy of Numbers 6

A Little History 8

Pythagoras, Father of Numerology 12

Misunderstood Numbers 14

Chapter 3: How to Use This Book 16

Using Correspondents 18

Colors, Gems, Crystals, and Vegetation 19

Food 20

Music Notes, Appeals, and Instruments 22

Chapter 4: How to Find Your Numbers: Challenge Number 23

Inside a Cask 24

Find the Numbers: Challenge 25

Instructions for the Number Table: Challenge 25

Number: Challenge System 26

The Number Time: Challenge Time 29

Categories of Personality 29

Basic Rules for Name Interpretation 30

Categories of Personality: Purpose and Instructions 31

Automation 31

Self-Image 31

Self-Expression 32

The Numbers Have a Positive Side and a Negative Side 33

Destination Number: Purpose and Instructions 34

Instructions for Finding the Number of the Destination 35

The Number of the Personal Year: Purpose and Instructions 36

Personal Year Number 1 37

Personal Year Number 2 37

Personal Year Number 3 38

Personal Year Number 4 38

Personal Year Number 5 38

Personal Year Number 6 38

Personal Year Number 7 38

Personal Year Number 8 39

Personal Year Number 9 39

Instructions to Find Your Personal Year 39

Method 1: Using Personal Year Quadriculates 39

Method 2: Using System Year 39

Numerical Comparisons 41

Chapter 5: Number 1 – Independence 45

Attributes 45

Correspondents 45

Challenges of the Number 1 47

Physical Challenges of the Number 1 48

Balancing the Challenges of the Number 1 50

Automotive 51

Self-Image 52

Self-Expression 53

Destiny 54

Personal Year 54

Personal Month 55

Personal Day 56

Chapter 6: Number 2 – Cooperation 57

Attributes 57

Correspondents 57

Challenges of the Number 2 59

Physical Challenges of the Number 2 60

Balancing the Challenges of the Number 2 62

Automotive 62

Self-Image 64

Self-Expression 65

Destiny: 66

Personal Year 66

Personal Month 67

Personal Day 67

Chapter 7: Number 3 – Communication 69

Attributes 69

Correspondents 69

Challenges of the Number 3 70

Physical Challenges of the Number 3: 71

Balancing the challenges of the Number 3 72

Self-Image 72

Self-Expression 73

Destiny: 74

Personal Year 74

Personal Month 75

Personal Day 76

Chapter 8: Number 4 – Practicality 78

Attributes 78

Correspondents 78

Challenges of the Number 4 80

Physical Challenges of the Number 4 81

Balancing the Challenges of the number 4 82

Automotive 83

Self-Image 84

Self-Expression 85

Destiny 86

Personal Year 87

Personal Month 88

Personal Day 88

Chapter 9: Number 5 – Sexual Freedom 90

Attributes 90

Correspondents 90

Challenges of the Number 5 92

Physical Challenges of the Number 5 93

Balancing The Challenge Of Number 5 94

Automotive 95

Self-Image 96

Self-Expression 97

Destiny 98

Personal Year 98

Personal Month 99

Personal Day 100

Chapter 10: Number 6 – Formation 101

Attributes 101

Correspondents 101

Challenges Of The Number 6 102

Physical Challenges of the Number 6 104

Balancing the Challenges of the Number 6 105

Automotive 105

Self-Image 107

Self-Expression 108

Destiny 109

Personal Year 109

Personal Month 110

Personal Day 111

Chapter 11: Number 7 – Mental Analysis 112

Attributes 112

Correspondents 112

Challenges of the Number 7 113

Physical Challenges of the Number 7 116

Balancing the Challenges of the Number 7 118

Automotive 119

Self-Image 123

Self-Expression 125

Destiny 128

Personal Year 128

Personal Month 130

Personal Day 131

Chapter 12: Number 8 – Material Power 132

Attributes 132

Correspondents 132

Challenges of the Number 8 134

Physical Challenges of the Number 8 135

Balancing the Challenges of the Number 8 136

Automotive 137

Self-Image 139

Self-Expression 139

Destiny: 141

Personal Year 141

Personal Month 142

Personal Day 143

Chapter 13: Number 9 And 0 – Conclusions 144

Attributes 144

Correspondents 144

The Challenges of the Numbers 9 and 0 145

Physical Challenges of the Numbers 9 and 0 147

Balancing the Challenges of the Numbers 9 and 0 148

Automotive 149

Self-Image 150

Self-Expression 152

Destiny 154

Personal Year 154

Personal Month 155

Personal Day 155

Conclusion 157

Introduction

Congratulations on purchasing *Numerology: Decoding Your Destiny,* and thank you for doing so.

There are plenty of books on this subject on the market, thanks again for choosing this one! Every effort was made to ensure it is full of as much useful information as possible. Please enjoy!

Are you on a search for a new dimension? A means of evaluating personal resources? If you can count on your fingers, you can easily use Numerology to find your answers. Numerology is a mystical arithmetic system that reveals character, personality, and experience through the sensitive progression of numbers.

Numerology's simple arithmetic bases its surprising revelations on more than 11,000 years of coincidence, and its effectiveness was recognized by the prehistoric, the ancient Greeks, and the societies of the Elizabethan era. Modernized in the sixth century BC, today it is a fast, simple, and positive system for self-examination and mapping of opportunities.

Numerology prolongs myopic vision, magnifies vision in the dark, and simply emits light when we need clarity. Numbers are not just cumulative values to be totalized by a calculator or applied to the probability of the data set. We are in the era of numbers, and the duality of its importance is increasingly in focus. We are attracted to people, places, and things that vibrate with us, and most of the time, we have one or two numbers that give us luck or appear to always appear in addresses and phone numbers, no matter how often we move. When you understand the essence of numerical meanings, you can then understand the kinds of people and experiences that you continually attract when you change your residence, telephone, and automobile.

Chapter 1: What is Numerology?

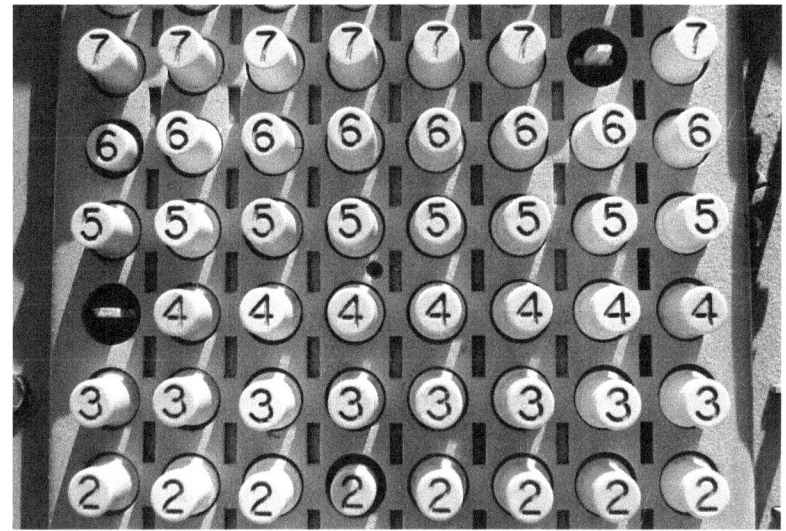

For those interested in metaphysics, Numerology can sharpen the techniques of mental expansion and prepare the mind to employ extra-sensory perceptions and mental transference easily. Numerology instigates the enlargement of the imagination. You can visualize your appearance, your sensations, and your actions, to the maximum of your potential, based on the meanings of the numbers. The ancients knew, and today's prognosticators believe that it is possible to conquer what the mind is able to visualize.

Numerology provides a complete profile of the lifestyle associated with personality when we apply the meanings of the individual numbers to the name we receive at birth and the date we are born. The numbers in our name describe the things we were born to know. The date numbers of our birth describe the things we have to learn.

The numerical symbols of the letters in your name sketch out your instincts, self-image, and natural talents. People immediately relate to their names.

Metaphysicians believe that the soul selects its name before birth to reflect the sound of its capabilities. To the listener, the name is the melody of the person, to which the souls respond favorably when pronounced. Names attract or repel according to the vibrations they emit. If you compare the numbers of the names of good friends and great lovers, you will find the same numbers in their respective numerological tables. Unpleasant relationships will present numbers that are not compatible. This is because, according to Pythagoras, the father of modern Numerology, "equal" numbers have a mutual affinity. Certain numbers that spring up continuously in someone's life, such as addresses, phone books, car plates, bank accounts, and social security numbers, come from their own name or date of birth. Your birth date numbers describe the experiences of life and your goals. The subdivisions of the date of birth—the day, month and year numbers—are symbols of three main cycles of life experiences, and the meaning of the total number explains the kind of people and experiences you will encounter on the way, also called destiny.

The meanings of the month and day of birth describe acts and attitudes. The meaning of the month of the birth number describes the impressions and environments of youth. The day-of-birth numbers symbolize the experiences of the 27-year cycle of midlife productivity, including the period from about 28 to 36 years of age, as you mature and stabilize. The birthday number is useful at this time because it focuses on your career and explains the options. In addition, there's the challenge number. I consider this number, found by subtracting your birth numbers, one of the most important in a person's life because it describes how you will live with your destiny. It tells you how to use your natural instincts and talents (symbolized by your birth name number) and how to deal with the people and experiences you encounter (symbolized by your birth date number).

And, finally, it is not your destiny, but your attitude that will determine success or failure, happiness or misfortune. When you use Numerology as a common-sense companion, everything becomes possible. You want to explore the greater meaning of your character, unveil disruptive habits, and gain perspective,

NUMEROLOGY will answer all your questions.

Chapter 2: The Philosophy of Numbers

We believe in the inexplicable when we say, "he is number one." Why was a person "dressed in nines" when he got along? Why are we "at six and seven" when in conflict? Why is it said that cats have only seven lives? Why not 10 or 17? Is there a numerological explanation for the "seven-year crisis"? Of course, there is. When you know the meanings of numbers, these superstitions make sense.

In order to form a basic ground for the meanings of the numbers, let's take a look at the evolution of the numbers from 1 to 9. Pythagoras believed that the numbers from 1 to 9 led to perfection, symbolized by the number 10. Here's how it works:

- We start with 1, the idea that develops in predictable progression, step by step.
- The number 2 symbolizes the idea of opening up, being received by others, and receiving the collaboration necessary to continue to develop.
- Number 3 carries the idea to others for inspection and approval.

- The number 4 leads the idea to practical application and corrects the impracticalities.
- Number 5 adds to the promotion and exposure to public opinion. Five, the central number, opens the door to unexpected advantages and disadvantages. Here, the idea makes the transition from individual concept to community consciousness.
- The number 6 is the symbol of group participation and community responsibility. It extends the concept to serve a greater purpose.
- The number 7 is the symbol of trimming the edges, of questioning and perfecting the idea, technically, until it becomes an important material result.
- Number 8 represents the life force, mental and physical organization, and practical power. It brings together body, mind, and spirit in order to produce tangible results. Ideas are formed through planning, work, and structure, applied during the influence of a number 8.
- Number 9 gives the polish, develops the skills necessary to bring the idea to the broader market, and concludes the process.

This process relates to everything we do. Ambitions develop through activities or experiences indicated by the meanings of numbers. The stages of development during the nine

months of pregnancy and the final perfection of the fetus in the ninth month are a prime example of the evolution of the numbers from 1 to 9. The birth of a child initiates a new life a few days after the conclusion of the ninth month. The child, a new concept, initiates the life cycle at birth and again at the beginning of the tenth month. In Numerology, the number 10 becomes a number 1, when we add 1 + 0, which results in 1. The pregnancy ends in the ninth month—9, the number of the terms. Life begins at number 1—the number of beginnings.

A Little History

Since 14,000 BC, when the Cro-Magnon man walked through the glaciers, people perceive, feel, and respond to the vibrations of numbers. Cavemen showed their interpretation of the duality of numbers with primitive designs on the floor and cave walls. The elders or leaders of cave clans gave rise to the mystery behind the counting system by refusing to expose their knowledge. The magic of numbers, as important as healing techniques, was transmitted only to the clan's most trusted and intelligent members. While crawling on the mental plane, when primeval man socialized himself, interacting with others for agriculture and barter, he probably developed counting by comparing a four-legged animal to the skins of four animals. However, the language was primitive, and the man had to create sounds for numbers. He used words that allied themselves with the examples observed in his natural environment.

Primal man developed pictorial words for the numbers. The name of a six-petalled flower may have been the symbol of the word that indicated the cumulative value of six. The drawings "were worth a thousand words, which did not exist in his vocabulary."

Man's ability to communicate was limited, but he could calculate. To indicate that he had three wives, a caveman could draw a female shape next to a three-edged sheet. The observers in the clan retained the drawings and used them repeatedly. As in the children's play of the cordless phone, in which the word changes as it is passed on, it also changes the meaning intended by the original artist of the caves. The use of symbols and the perception of the meanings of their combinations led to the mystical aspects of cumulative symbols (numbers) that indicated more than their obvious quantity.

Numerology, as used today, incorporates the research, imagination, and intellectual idealizations of these and other ancient societies. Around 3000 BC, the Sumerians established the sophisticated numerical system that gave us the hour of 60 minutes and the minute of 60 seconds. His knowledge was transmitted to the Babylonians, who refined it. Modern Numerology began with the Greek civilizations of the sixth century BC. All the ancients (Sumerians, Babylonians and Chaldeans, later Pythagoras and Plato, and later Renaissance believers) believed that the basic elements of tone, idea, and thought had a mathematical basis. Early Christian art was informed, through Numerology, with the Byzantine application of the six as the perfect number of creation. Six animals, six edged objects, six birds in flight were found in mosaics and drawings from that era, symbolizing perfection. From the evolution of man from the primitive caves and the glaciers until around 632 BC and the establishment of the numerological system of Pythagoras, different numbers provoked new concepts. The Tarot cards, for example, precursors of the modern deck, are based on a pictorial and numerical system. The reading of the letters began when humans conceptualized intimate consciousness, built self-control, and tried to master fate. The pictorial interpretation began with a column of colored stones, which, in more sophisticated cultures, became mosaic tiles. The interpretation of colors, quantities, and images was inserted into a system based on coincidence—the repeated positions of the stones.

What the origin of the numerical charts or when they materialized in the form of collection or deck is not known. In archaeological digs, Egyptian, Jewish, Mexican, Indian, and Chinese archaeological excavations were found tarot decks, mosaic murals, and sculptures depicting the 22 pictorial letters that comprised the main arcana of the neurological system. They were tools for evaluating character and for prediction. What they said was whispered from teacher to pupil. Leaders protected the mystical power that instilled fear in ordinary citizens.

It was the Jewish people, devoted to the idea of preserving tradition, which preserved the purity of Tarot meanings. The keys of the Old Testament's Egyptian-Hebrew scriptures in the Books of Moses (far more complex than the card reader supposes) are understood only by the Talmudic scholars who link the numbers of the Tarot to the Kabbalah. The Kabbalah has the key to the place of the unknown vowel, necessary for interpretation. Twenty-two numbers and letters describe the primitive Hebrew alphabet. Each row of letters is also a row of numbers that sum up word, name, or expression, revealing the complexity of the Pentateuch, the Jewish writing. To this day, Jews greatly value knowledge and continue to study numbers. And thanks to the significance they give to the Kabbalistic interpretation of their scriptures we have the documentation of a part of the evolution that led to modern Numerology. But they were not the only ones to develop a system of drawings and numbers.

The Tarot number system was also used by European gypsies, who are believed to be of Egyptian or Hindu origin and did not receive their knowledge of the Jews. Egyptian priests, like other ancient hierarchies, used their knowledge of metaphysical techniques to increase control over others. They were arrogant, kept secrets, and inspired fear in the ignorant, which depended on the birthright or the survival of the fittest. The predictions were passed on to the leaders, who used Numerology to unseat and predict the actions of the enemy. There was a belief (some say also in Pythagoras) that the Egyptians and the Orientals went back to Atlantis and that from there came the knowledge of magic. Could Pythagoras have learned the "divine knowledge" and the perfections of Numerology when he traveled as a young man? Fable or truth? Impossible to say, because these primitive beliefs were hidden by religious secrecy and by maneuvers of power.

We know that with Taro, the desire to understand self-image with drawings and numbers began. The interpretation changed over time and according to the society in which it was used. When writing began, numerical figures may have been drawn from a visual or a finger—the mental picture of the purpose of 1. For example, number 1, graphically, is standing without leaning on anything, alone. It is not difficult to understand that the numerological interpretation "independence" was applied to type 1 personality or destiny. Force the imagination and put yourself in the place of the ancients, who have been trying to make sense of things that cannot be touched, tasted, smelled, heard, seen, or spent. See how easy it would be to associate number 1 with the character of an independent person. Life opens to some number 1 destination if independence is assimilated. Challenge 1 requires a person to balance their independent actions. Could it be possible for Numerology to be born?

Systems continued to differ according to religious beliefs until Pythagoras began his Greek school of mystery. His religious belief was based on the scientific and mathematical understanding of the relation of universal truths to numbers.

Pythagoras, Father of Numerology

It was the charismatic Pythagoras of Samos, born in 580 BC, who dedicated his serene genius to calling forms and ideas by numbers. In an era in which humans and gods interacted, it was natural that, after his enlightening journeys around the world, Pythagoras would draw and conquer followers. It was his intention to elevate the man from 1 (egocentrism) to 9 (stripping). The nature of his evaluations and conclusions led Pythagoras—and later came to inspire Jesus of Nazareth—to convey to third parties the assimilated knowledge of various foreign cultures. He integrated mathematics, music, mysticism, science, astronomy, and philosophy, using them as the basis of his practical applications. Over time, he founded a religion, with school and everything, that gave support to its principles.

Revered as "the master," as "that man," Pythagoras led his followers to a "way of living." He was troubled by the thought that words did not bring a proper understanding of concepts and objects, which could be better described, he believed, by numbers.

The works of Pythagoras were transmitted by respectable disciples. In the form of texts, either they were lost, or they did not exist. His convictions and theories had an impact on the teachings of Plato, St. Thomas Aquinas, St. Augustine, Aristotle, and

Francis Bacon. There were many Greek mystery schools, but none studied, disciplined, and educated every potential disciple with the same care of Pythagoras. His school experienced human relationships and inspired, in the disciples, for many centuries, lasting loyalty.

Misunderstood Numbers

Should we refuse the extra thread in the baker's dozen to avoid a disgrace? The 13 is considered, without reason, evil. Thirteen sat down at the table of Jesus Christ for the  Last Supper and followed one death. Was it to risk fate, running the risk of someone dying, sitting 13 people at a dinner table? It is rare to find the thirteenth floor in apartment buildings. But what is 13, if not 1 + 12?

For the numerologist, the 13 indicates transformation. It presages, in general, the uprising and the decline that lead to the reconstruction at a higher level. When Judas, the thirteenth at the table of Christ, began the acts that led to the crucifixion of Jesus, inaugurated the cycle of rebirth and evolution of universal Christianity. He took Christ's philosophy out of the kitchen and put it into the world. The thirteenth guest created public outcry that galvanized the followers of the entire universe. It is true that death occurred after the thirteenth sitting at the table, but the higher self of Christ lives from the religious, practical, and structured belief organized by his converts.

Thirteen is just a probation number that drives humanity to heights or depths. Numbers 13, 14, 16, and 19 are not evil but provocative. According to Christian belief, Jesus lived according to the common and basic values of honesty, truth, and love. It is said that it worked for the sake of the constructive good and did not fall prey to superficial and egocentric values (the meanings of 1 and 3, which make 13). The 13, in the numerological table, indicates proof of faith in life. It is a test of the number of its sum, 4 (13 = 1 + 3 = 4). Therefore, Numerology believes that the number 13 draws successes and failures that lead to an ordeal of economy, self-discipline, and positivity—with emphasis on work. The number 13 requires practicality, good judgment, and dedication to work for constructive values. Person number 13 always has reconstruction options.

The 13th was divine and powerful to the ancients. It is a number misunderstood nowadays, simply explainable as an exceptional number of influences, which requires the simple and objective desire to ignore superficial values and frivolity. Numerology always provides reasonable explanations for numbers that have historically been the focus of attention.

Chapter 3: How to Use This Book

- To learn the basics of Numerology, prepare to make numerological tables with the following tools in hand:

    a) Rubber pencil

    b) The draft paper for sums

    c) Add-on machine or calculator if you prefer not to add on your fingers or mentally.

- Begin by finding the uni digital number for each of the five categories of your life (challenge, automation, self-image, self-expression, and destiny).

- Write the uni digital numbers of the categories in the list of numerological categories.

- Read the meanings of the appropriate category number, listed in the chapter on the meanings of this book.

- Write down the correspondents for each of your category numbers and read how to use them in the corresponding sections.

- To analyze a personal table: compare the meanings of the challenge number with the meanings of the numbers of the most categories. Use the number-challenge meanings to identify pitfalls. Use personality categories to confirm self-knowledge. Use the destination descriptions to predict the options.
- To analyze and compare two tables: compare the category numbers to establish compatibility. Refer to the generic compatibility or incompatibility numbers listed under the corresponding.

First, learn the numerical values of the alphabet. Make at least 10 complete maps for friends and family. Record the meanings of the category numbers for each map in the book on a tape recorder. Forget the sound of your voice if it is not to your liking. Your listeners are only concerned with the words you will say about them. Be friendly. Enter the person's name. If you find something interesting or funny, demonstrate it. When you feel solidarity, demonstrate in the voice.

Read the categories of personality, destination, personal year (the current year) and the personal month (the current month), in that order. Leave the meanings of the challenge to the end.

Give Numerology ribbons for engagement, divorce, or birthday gifts. You will receive positive feedback that will bring you self-confidence. The more tapes you make, the more you want to do. Repeating the reading of numeric meanings will help you remember. Decorating should not be a problem. Get into the habit of adding mentally. The key is to visualize the column of numbers before attempting to add.

Remember that 9, plus any number will keep the reduced number unchanged; therefore, it is unnecessary to add 9. Think of the name "Virlis". (V) 4 + (L) 3 + (S) 1 = 8. If we deal with I, R and I (all 9), we would have 4 + 9 + 9 + 3 + 9 + 1 = 35, and 3 + 5 = 8, however.

Using Correspondents

At the beginning of each chapter of the meanings of a number, you will find things that have vibrations corresponding to that particular number. There are letters, colors, foods, crystals, vegetation, instruments, and musical notes that will be familiar or receptive to people who have the same numerical vibrations in their self-motivation, self-image, self-expression, or destiny. Correspondents will be valuable during years, months, and personal days that share the same numbers. When challenge numbers match correspondents, these objects detonate emotional responses.

In general, people are attracted automatically by their own numeric correspondents. It is not necessary to surround yourself with jewelry, food, colors, or music that match the numbers on your table or avoid the things that are challenges. However, your daily life can be energized with the presence of corresponding non-challenges in the immediate vicinity. Challenge objects can be corrosive.

Your correspondents appear to require actions or reactions if they match the numbers on your map. When you use, eat, listen to, or reside with objects or places with your numbers, you are creating your personal environment and focusing on the people or experiences that make your life more fruitful and relaxed.

Colors, Gems, Crystals, and Vegetation

Colors, gems, crystals, and vegetation can be used to determine moods and attract help. Those that correspond to your personal numbers complement you, and you should use them in the decoration of the house to give serenity, to invite like spirits, or to provide pleasant activities. For example, a turquoise ring on a person's token number 5 sends a subliminal invitation to people who have the number 5 in their personality numbers, destination numbers or their mutant numbers for the year, month, and day.

Color, gem, crystal, or vegetation that match your target number should NOT be used unless you are modifying behavior and have achieved a certain balance in your personality and life. When using a correspondent challenge, expect to attract people and experiences that emotionally react to practical situations — using match-defying decorating sets challenging moods.

Color, gem, crystal, or vegetation corresponding to your self-motivation number should be used at home or when relaxing. They will attract people or experiences that leave you at ease. Your self-image correspondent should be used as an effect to improve the first impression. Your self-correspondent expression should be used to support self-expression and professional ambitions. Your destination correspondent should be used to attract new people and experiences that teach the meaning of the destination number. Using color, gem, crystal or vegetation that matches your personal year, month or day attracts people or experiences that highlight the meaning of these numbers. Use red on day number 1 to send self-affirming vibration. It is interesting to note that, without planning, on personal day 1, many people instinctively use red color.

Food

"We are what we eat," numerologically. Foods that match challenge numbers can cause indigestion. Either you overeat them to taste them, or you avoid them—there is no balance in your attitude-related attitudes. In certain cases, challenge food numbers can improve your health.

For example, if people who have the number 1 challenge avoid eating the number 1 food, such as boiled beans, lobster, or chocolate, they may improve or eliminate their problems with diarrhea, cellulitis, or hernia.

If you eat foods that match personality numbers, the effect on health will be protective. The destination numbers present you with the corresponding foods—which will be offered to you, and you will want to learn about them. Mutant tastes can be identified by personal year, month, and day numbers. Foods that match your self-motivation number can be combined with other foods corresponding to the personality number. Try to use their correspondents to support the respective categories: self-help food for relaxation, self-image food to support first impressions, food self-expression in combination with the talents, food of the destination for new experiences.

Music Notes, Appeals, and Instruments

It is said that music calms the wild mood. You will find pleasure in musical correspondences related to your numbers of self-motivation, self-image, and self-expression. Correspondents of challenge numbers can be aggressive and generate emotional responses that accelerate or delay behavior modification. If you listen to the melody of your favorite romantic song, you may shed tears of depression or tears of joy. You will love or hate the challenge of musical correspondents, and you may want to use them to create a mood that puts you in touch with your feelings. Of people who cannot stand the time needed to follow their emotions and search for the reasons why they are followed by melancholy, the musical correspondents of the challenge may be valuable to the therapist treating them.

Chapter 4: How to Find Your Numbers: Challenge Number

This Numerology book emphasizes challenging numbers whose impact, importance, and value have not been addressed or explained in depth. Numerology gives the descriptions of challenge numbers' greater importance than the descriptions of personality numbers and fate. So, before looking up your personality and destination numbers, find your challenge numbers.

Challenge users should also read the other categories (self-motivation, self-image, etc.!) to find their challenge numbers. They may be helpful in attempting to "grate" the black and white views of the challenging aspect of the number. When a challenge number is the same as that of the personality category, derived from the name or day of birth, it points to exact areas of the personality that need to balance the destination. When challenge numbers do not appear in other categories of personality, it is because they touch every aspect of personality.

- Challenges are best understood by the person whose name and day of birth are being mapped. They are tools for self-analysis—keys to honest self-evaluations.
- Challenges are rooted in childhood experiences. After maturity, they manifest themselves in symptoms that cloud logic and create exaggerated emotional reactions.
- Challenges are the hidden motives behind repeated mistakes and emotional extremes. They describe personality attributes that are used on the positive or negative ends. The bearer of a challenge lacks points of reference in childhood that indicate balanced behavior.
- Challenges explain the reason that you have many options. You can see a glass of water half full or half empty.
- Challenges show how to face fate. It is the attitudes of a person, not destiny, that generate success or disappointment.

"The target is the sum of reactions to our actions. So we have to change so that the target also changes" – Elisabeth Haich

Inside a Cask

There are nine types of challenges, each symbolized by one of the numbers from 1 to 9. Personal challenge numbers are found by means of a subtraction routine of the date of birth. The number-challenge meanings describe the cause, effect, and cure of inappropriate adult habits, based on the child's emotional view. These habits cause stress and affect how we face the bitter and destructive displays of black and white opinions and deeds. The gray tones of constructive commitment are illusory because they are the unknowns of childhood. The number-challenge meanings fill many gaps in our childhood and open our eyes toward happier maturity.

Find the Numbers: Challenge

Numerology has a basic rule. All double numbers are added together and reduced to a unique number, adding from left to right.

Example:

45 = 4 + 5 = 9

34 = 3 + 4 = 7

28 is captious and requires two steps.

28 = 2 + 8 = 10;

1 + 0 = 1;

Therefore, 28 becomes 1 in Numerology. The zero has a mean value, equivalent to 9, which is described in the meanings of the chapter of number 9.

Instructions for the Number Table: Challenge

Overall Step 1: Look for the day, month, and year of birth to find the challenge numbers.

Step 1. Convert the month of birth into number by finding its place in the calendar.

January = 1, February = 2, March = 3, April = 4, May = 5, June = 6, July = 7, August = 8, September = 9, October = 1, November = 2, December = 3

Step 2. Reduce birth year to a unique number.

Example: 1937 = 2

Add 1 + 9 + 3 + 7 = 20 and reduce the unique number. 2 + 0 = THE YEAR 1937 = 2

1954 = 1

So, 1 + 9 + 5 + 4 = 19, and reduce the unique number. 1 + 9 = 10 and 1 + 0 = THE YEAR 1954 = 1

Number: Challenge System

Step 1. Fill in the unidentified numbers of the date of your birth:

A _____ B. _____ C _____

     Day   Month   Year

Note: Always subtract the smaller number from the larger number.

Step 2. B-A = _____ (Birth to 28 years of age)

Step 3. A—C = _____ (After 28 years of age)

Step 4. Subtract the remaining B-A from the rest of A-C: _____ All Life)

Step 5. B—C = _____ (All Life)

Example: July 12, 1937, is the date of birth of Bill Cosby.

12 (1 + 2) is added and becomes 3 = 3

July is the 7th the month of the calendar = 7

1937 = 1 + 9 + 3 + 7 = 20, and 2 + 0 = 2

Step 1. Bill Cosby's birth date with numbers: 3 (day) 7 (month) 2 (year)

Step 2 7-3 = 4; his biggest focus is on youth and middle age.

Step 3. 3-2 = 1; your biggest focus is on middle age and beyond.

Step 4. 4-1 = 3; the focus is on lifetime.

Step 5. 7-2 = 5; the focus is on lifetime.

The challenges of Bill Cosby's birth date are 4, 1, 3, and 5.

Example: 1st June 1926, the date of birth of Marylin Monroe.

Step 1. Birthday date with numbers: 1 (day) 6 (month) 9 (year)

(1 + 9 + 2 + 6 = 18; 1 + 8 = 9)

Step 2. 6—1 = 5 of the month and day)

Step 3. 9—1 = 8

Step 4. 8—5 = 3

Step 5. 9—6 = 3

The challenges of Marylin Monroe's birth date were 5, 8, 3, and 3.

The Number Time: Challenge Time

Note that Marylin Monroe has double challenge numbers. Marylin Monroe has the 3, socially insecure, and jealous of her own image. When a challenge number appears more than once, the challenge is hard to beat. The dual challenge numbers warn that influences or environments of childhood will not change with maturity. These challenges are constantly being reinforced. It is more desirable that the challenge holder digest them gradually over a long period of time. Situations will arise to focus on their meanings.

Overall, Step 2. FIRST CHALLENGE: The subtraction of the month and day gives the number that describes the challenge felt most strongly until around the twenty-eighth birthday.

Overall, Step 3. SECOND CHALLENGE: The subtraction of the day and year gives the number that describes the challenge felt most strongly in the middle, which can last and arrive until the last years.

Overall Steps 4 and 5. THREE AND FOURTH CHALLENGES: Subtractions from the remains of the day and year require lifelong attention.

Categories of Personality

Personality is divided into three categories—self-motivation, self-image, and self-expression. You'll find the categories numbers of your personality, using the full birth name.

Basic Rules for Name Interpretation

To construct a map, use only the exact letters of the names printed on the birth certificate or equivalent. Nominations, baptismal names, early name changes, wedding names, and professional names should not be used in the construction of the numerological map.

Junior, Son, Grandson, etc. are not included in the name map. It is accepted that the child will have the characteristics of the name, which were the same for the first owner of the name. Uniqueness is explained through the opportunities offered by different names at birth.

Being a newborn, a boy, a girl, a teenager, a man or a woman, an initial (A., B., C. etc.) or a name that was never used but was registered in the birth certificate or album (the family Bible etc.) of any culture, will be the name to be used in the preparation of the numerological map. It is understood that the first record has been chosen by the new soul who came to earth to fulfill its purposes.

Note: There are all sorts of logical reasons to call this numerological rule impossible, ridiculous, and crazy, and many customers have already told me, "But I never used this name ... it was a mistake." However, the para-scientists, the metaphysicians, and the numerologists believe that there is a purpose and a plan for all. There are no mistakes.

Categories of Personality: Purpose and Instructions

Automation

Your self-motivation number is derived from the numerical values of the vowels of your full name of birth. Use the name that appears on the birth certificate or another first record according to the custom of different countries and cultures. The numerical equivalents of the full-name vowels, summed up and reduced to a single number, reveal what we want, what we feel inclined, and what we want to have to feel content. Instinctively, we dedicate our body and soul to the values described by the number of our self-motivation. It describes what we want to be and what we want from our lives.

To add depth and scope to the understanding of the self-motivation number, you should also read the numerical meaning of each individual name of the full birth name. The reduced single number of vowels of the first name indicates the practical instincts. The reduced single number of the vowels of the first surname (s) describes the emotional instincts. The reduced number of vowels in the last surname reveals the spiritual instincts of the bearer and the paternal side of the family. Self-motivation, on the metaphysical plane, is called "impetus of the soul."

Self-Image

Your self-image number is derived from the numerical values of the consonants of your birth name. The unique number calculated for your full name is the most important. However, the numbers of the individual names of a birth name add to the understanding of what we want to show the world.

The self-image number reveals the impression that observers have of us when we step out of an elevator, thinking no one notices us, or when we enter a room without being announced—it is the first impression we make. And the visualization of the success that we cherished when we were young when we dreamed and planned the way we walk, talk, dress, and progress as adults.

When we live according to the meanings of our self-image number, we disregard the demands of others and emit, in their place, numerical vibrations that attract our dreams. Our self-image is born in the imagination. And the key to understanding how we see ourselves at our best.

Self-Expression

Your self-expression number is derived from the sum of all numeric values of the letters of the full name. The numbers of each name are totalized separately and reduced to a number. These numbers are then summed and reduced to a number. To find the overall picture, read the meaning of the value of the unique number of all letters. Individual names in the full name of birth, when reduced to the meaning of their unique number, describe talents, potentials, and methods of self-expression. The meanings of the reduced unique numbers of first names, first names, and surnames of the full birth name should be read for the purpose of obtaining additional information.

The number of self-expression indicates your professional talents and sums up their capabilities. Its ingredients suggest professional choices that use material capabilities. Whether as a homemaker, hobbyist, or a dedicated professional, you'll be more comfortable concentrating on the meanings of self-expression numbers with the goal of attracting recognition.

The Numbers Have a Positive Side and a Negative Side

The numerological map must be completed before reading the individual meanings of the numbers because all the complex parts of our nature must be viewed as a whole. In order to fully understand a numerological profile of the personality and its destiny, we must recognize that every numerical description has a negative side and a positive side. Most people are not always positive or negative, might not even be balanced a number of times.

The complexities in our nature become clear when the meanings of our numbers are read one after the other. People are not simple. We often confuse our friends and ourselves by revealing conflicting desires. A complete personality map sheds light on these dichotomies.

After reading all the personal numerical values, new options for us will appear. The possibilities, hitherto unplanned, indicated by a number of the personality category, might send flames on the Scarlet O'Haras who are among us and who "leave for tomorrow what they can do today." The definition of periods of life can detonate a sense of immediacy. Scrutinizing opportunities for life can ease the worries of those who believe that life is surpassing them.

We pack, very often, in the events of the moment. Our past efforts and our aspirations for the future may lock in when we think we are facing an emergency. It is human to clear the numerical meanings of Numerology in order to find solutions to the immediate problems, but it is better to return to the long-term possibilities indicated by the description of our destination number as soon as the emergency is over.

Numerology helps us understand when and how time can heal our emotional wounds or solve problems. If we wait to read the numeric meanings of the entire list of personality categories, we may discover new predicates. It may be that, for the future, there is a very well-defined chronology of events. There may be a more promising solution that reduces anxiety and gives less importance to what may appear to be a need for immediate action.

In order to benefit from the side view offered by Numerology, it is best to map first and read later.

Destination Number: Purpose and Instructions

The destination number describes what they expect us to learn. Metaphysically speaking, the number of destiny describes our purpose on the plane of life. The types of person and experience  indicated by this number will not be surprising unless the traits of self-motivation, self-image, and self-expression of the personality, or the date of birth, are the same.

If the self-expression number is the same as the destination number early in life, you will have a profession, and the experiences you encounter will accelerate your progress. If your self-motivation number is the same as the destination number, you will quickly get to know the people and experiences that will make you feel better. If your self-image number is the same as your destination number, you will have opportunities to experience the fantasies of the life you led as a child.

Few people have the same numbers in the categories of personality and destiny. Most people live the "seek-and-find" method and learn from experience. By understanding the numerological meaning of the destination number, you are able to identify who you will become, what you are expected to do when the time comes, why you are here, after all, where you should seek help, and when things happen at the right time.

Instructions for Finding the Number of the Destination

Step 1: Add the numbers of the day, month, and year of birth. Or reduce the day, month, and year numbers to unique numbers, and add them.

Step 2: Reduce the sum to a number between 1 and 9. The unique reduced number of the sum of the numbers of the day, month, and year of birth is the destination number.

Bill Cosby's example: July 12, 1937

12 = 1 + 2 = 3

July = 7

1937 = 1 + 9 + 3 + 7 = 20; and 2 + 0 = 2

3 + 7 + 2 = 12; and 1 + 2 = 3

OR

12 + 7 + 1937 = 1956; and 1 + 9 + 5 + 6 = 21; and 2 + 1 = 3

The destination number of Bill Cosby is 3.

The Number of the Personal Year: Purpose and Instructions

Life is divided into cycles of nine years of experience. We begin new concepts in the personal year of the cycle and conclude the goal of the first cycle eight years later in a personal year number 9. The seven years between years 1 and 9 give our initial concept. In the personal year number 9, we leave the past and prepare ourselves for a new course in the following year—the personal year number 1 that begins another cycle of experiences. It is said that we live in cycles of seven years, but few remember factoring the first year when ideas take shape, or the last year when we abandon the idea.

During personal year number 9, we reflected on the past eight years and found that personal year number 1 goals were met. New concepts are born based on achievements or conclusions. The seed of change is planted. You cannot start and finish important projects in the same year; so when the year 9 is over, new things are instigated in a year 1. They are cultivated in a 2, they come to light in a 3, they descend to earth in a 4, they make transitions in a 5, they add responsibilities in a 6, they specialize in a 7, make material advances in an 8, and achieve recognition in a 9.

Each year of the nine-year cycle has a purpose.

Personal Year Number 1

Offers opportunities for change in the direction of progress. It's a start-up year, during which we can expect to start projects.

Personal Year Number 2

Offers opportunities to know the details of projects initiated in cycle number 1. And a year of details, receptive, during which we build the future results.

Personal Year Number 3

Offers opportunities to bring to light the goals of cycle number 1. And a year of start-up, during which we can expect to see the results of social contacts.

Personal Year Number 4

Offers opportunities to correct bad practices and build security for the future. It is a year of work, receptive, during which we build for the future.

Personal Year Number 5

Offers opportunities to try new ideas, to use various means of self-promotion, and to experience physical pleasures. And a year of start-up, transformer, during which we can expect to see results. The first four cycles of the personal year are rooted in independent acts. The fifth-year is a central cycle that opens the door to unknowns and the transition of the way of life.

Personal Year Number 6

Offers opportunities to conduct long-term intimate business and commitments, to take on obligations, and to be useful. It is a receptive year during which we build for the future.

Personal Year Number 7

Offers opportunities to be introspective and to re-evaluate intimate, business, and spiritual goals. And a solitary year, to observe, be receptive and expect little if any, commercial result.

Personal Year Number 8

Offers opportunities to take control of material and commercial matters. And a year of problem-solving, to be very aggressive, courageous and expect high-level tangible results.

Personal Year Number 9

Offers opportunities to be philosophical, worshipful, and charitable. It is a year to be receptive to the needs of many people, to set an example and expect the results of the original concepts shaped in the personal year number 1. And a year to clean the rotten. Nothing new begins.

Instructions to Find Your Personal Year

Method 1: Using Personal Year Quadriculates

Step 1: Look for the grid for the current calendar year.

Step 2: Look for the date of your birth (day and month) on the grid and find the number of your personal year.

Method 2: Using System Year

Step 1: First, you should look for a unique number for any calendar year. Add the calendar year numbers and reduce them to a number between 1 and 9.

EXAMPLE OF CALENDAR YEAR:

1991 = 1 + 9 + 9 + 1 = 20

2 + 0 = 2

1991 = Year of the Calendar Number 2

Step 2: Add the unique calendar year number to the numbers of your month and day of birth.

Step 3: Totals equal to or greater than 10 should be reduced to a one-digit number by adding their two digits.

Example: BILL COSBY PERSONAL YEAR FOR 1991

Date of birth: July 12

Step 1: 1991 = 1 + 9 + 9 + 1-20 -2 + 0 = 2

Step 2: Add 3 (12 = 1 + 2 = 3)

+ 7 (July, the seventh calendar month)

+ 2 (calendar year number)

TOTAL = 12 = 3

Bill Cosby is in a personal year number 3 in 1991.

Numerical Comparisons

There are several ways to use the numeric comparison on your own map or between two maps. For example, if you want to know if your talents are on a destination track that will offer  immediate recognition, compare your self-expression number with your destination number. If you want to know if it's compatible with a colleague or work superior, compare your self-expression number with his. If you want to know if your first impression is compatible with the people and experiences you will encounter in life, read the meaning of your self-image number and compare it to the focus of your destination number. Common sense always helps to make comparisons and determine compatibility.

The following is a quick numerical comparison table to identify the numbers that are generally compatible and those that are not. But, remember, Numerology always provides choice: incompatible numbers do not have to cause frictional relationships; it is enough that partners or partners understand each other and want to make a reciprocal commitment. They are levels of incompatibility that can be relieved with the commitment of both to work together. But the first step always depends on the person who has the smallest number. He or she will have to be willing to learn from the person who has the highest number. And whoever has the highest number should make a commitment to give the smallest person enough time to learn. Communication is the key. Same numeric meanings in your table and in someone else's chart can set the path to the best relationship. However, if you are thinking of starting a long-term commitment to a person whose self-motivation and destination numbers are incompatible with yours, it may be better to agree than to disagree before problems arise.

Here are some practical rules for comparing numbers:

- When plotting comparisons between maps or on your own map, always use the final reduced number of categories for the challenge, self-motivation, self-image, self-expression, destination, year, month, and day.

- On your own map, compare your desires (self-motivation) to your talents (self-expression) to find out if you have the talent to get what you want.

- On your own map, compare your self-expression (talents) number to that of your destination to see if you will find people and experiences that will make it easier for you to contact business or profession. If these numbers are incompatible, you should focus on the meaning of your destination number to know what kinds of environments will open doors for you.

- On your own map, compare your challenge numbers to your numbers of self-motivation, self-image, and self-expression. If they are the same, you can mark the extreme part of your personality that reaches extremes and needs modification. If one of your challenge numbers equals your destination number or personal year, month or day numbers, you will find it difficult to react to the people and experiences you encounter without putting emotion into practical situations. You can soften your life by understanding that your intense emotional reactions are detonated by the people your destination presents (you will not want to choose the wrong person to date, get married, or work). You can smoothen your life by focusing on locking relationships with people and experiences that will help you throughout the time or period in question.

- On your own map, if the single reduced number of your self-motivation is greater than your destination, this means that you want more comforts than life offers. If your self-image number is larger than your target number, you seem more accomplished than most people you meet. If your self-expression number is greater than your destination number, you have more talent than you need to fulfill your destiny. If your name numbers are less than your destination number, you need to strive to learn what life has to offer. Always remember that the numbers of self-motivation, self-image, and self-expression, referring to the name, relate to the character, and the challenge numbers, of the destination, of the year, month, and day, of birth, relate to the types of person and experience you can expect to encounter.

- When making comparisons between maps or on your own map, compare personal year numbers to month and day numbers to find out when months and days will support the purpose of the year and are not frustrating. When short periods do not lead to quick realizations, it is best to be prepared for delays and understand that the person worried about you are also experiencing difficulties.

- To determine when to enter into a partnership, a marriage, or a business, compare your personal year numbers. The number 9 is a year of terms and never starts anything that lasts. Number 6 is ideal. Whenever possible, aim to start a long-term commitment in year 6. If this seems impossible, choose to get married in a month or day number 6. In business, numbers 4 and 8 are fortunate as well. But do not start in a year, month, or day number 9. Also, be sure to read the meaning of the two partners' personal year to understand what the opportunities are.

- Always compare your personal day numbers with those of your close friends and co-workers. If you know when to be a good listener and when to give an opinion, you will effortlessly accomplish the goals of your personal day.

- The reduced single birth date can be compared between two maps to determine compatibility from approximately 28 to 55 years of age.
- Month-of-birth numbers can be compared between two maps to determine if early environments will offer clogs or unknowns, comfortable or uncomfortable reference points.

The tables of quick numerical comparisons are comfortable, but if you have the time, it is best to read the full numeric meanings and thus gain deeper intimate insights. When in doubt, or when you need to make a quick decision, use common sense. Numerology is a tool and a companion of struggle. Your yearly, monthly, or daily forecasts can teach you how to save time until you're sure you're doing the 'right' thing.

Chapter 5: Number 1 – Independence

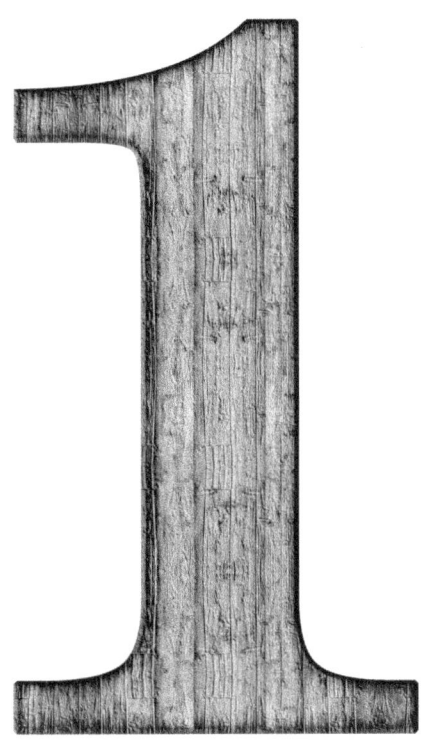

Attributes

Positive – Individuality, Leadership, Creativity, Positivity, Active Power, Ambition, Persistence, Self-confidence, audacity

Negative – Self-centeredness, authoritarianism, Imitation, Repression, Dependency, sloth, passivity, fear, weakness

Correspondents

LETTERS: A, J, and S

MENTAL AND PERSONAL ATTAINMENT NUMBERS:

10, 19, 28, 37, 46, 55, 64, 73, 82, 91, 100

COLOR: red

GEM: Ruby

CRYSTALS: Granada & Pyrite

VEGETATION: azalea, Iris, lilac

FOOD: Salad, Baked beans, Halibut, Lobster, Chocolate

MUSICAL INSTRUMENT AND/OR CALL: Piano, Opera

MUSICAL NOTE: Central

PLANET: The Sun

MONTHS: January to October

DAYS OF BIRTH: 1, 10, 19:28

DAY OF WEEK: Sunday

GENERAL COMPATIBILITY NUMBER (S): 3, 5, 9, 11, 22, 33

INCOMPATIBILITY NUMBERS: 6, 24

Note: If the individual has no 1 challenge number, these descriptions change from positive to negative until you balance the challenge. Make sure you read the meaning of the challenge.

Challenges of the Number 1

It is a challenge to the individual's self-respect. It is rooted in excessive control or very sensitive discipline by authority figures in childhood. In particular, the father was very little aggressive or was not present during the formation of the child. The mother, perhaps, was very authoritarian, playing the role of the "man" and confusing the child. Therefore, the child becomes an adult without understanding how to be comfortable alone or how to communicate to get what you want or need.

As the child grows, if independent ideas and decisions come up against criticism or overprotective worship, it will become frustrated and do things that are inappropriate for attention. You will try to please or annoy the incomprehensible parent or controlling authority. You will get into the habit of going from one end to the other. By not being able to autonomy, by wanting love, but not knowing how to satisfy personal expectations or desires, the child will be easily controllable, or angry, will try to control himself.

In youth, if the authority figure has shown excessive concern or was too inaccessible or unavailable by divorce or death, the child perceived acceptance or rejection as "he loves me, he does not love me." Infant emotional judgments, based on black and white perceptions, persist until maturity when challenges take effect. When experiencing creative ideas, when young, or emitting professional concepts as an adult, the bearer of the challenge expects to be received with disapproval or flattering exultation for utility and individualism.

Challenge number 1 can swing from one to the other of the following extremes, until each one of them is recognized, initiating new habits that stabilize the ego.

- Very impatient or very passive.
- Very independent or very dedicated.
- Very accomplished or very unpretentious.
- Very creative or very copier.
- Very ambitious or very lethargic.
- Very egocentric or very indulgent.
- Very aggressive or very indecisive.
- Very affirmative or very submissive.
- Very controllable or very controllable.
- Very obedient or very provocative.
- Very selfish or very generous.
- Very domineering or very obsequious.
- Very changeable or very lazy.

Physical Challenges of the Number 1

Challenges can affect physical as well as mental health. The chemistry of the body changes when individuals are stressed, and when we do not know what is good for us, our minds detonate anxious, angry, or frustrated habits. When we mistreat ourselves, we become sick. Every attitude sends a message to the brain, and the brain tells the body to scream for help.

To draw attention to their discomfort, people often become ill or form negative habits. Numerologists believe that illness and well-being depend on attitude, and challenges indicate attitudes resulting from feelings of need. When we do not feel needy, we feel good, balanced, and do not beg for the attention of others. Essentially, if personality challenges are balanced, the body's chemistry will remain balanced, too, and therefore, the risk of physical or mental illness will below.

Challenge numbers indicate the ways in which people punish themselves unconsciously for not being consciously good about themselves. The list of illnesses and negative habits to follow is related to the challenge of number 1.

- Anorexia Nervosa
- Urinating in Bed
- Bladder
- Bone problems
- Cellulite
- Circulatory Problem
- Cough
- Deafness
- Diarrhea
- Fever
- Foot Problems
- Glaucoma
- Headache

- Hernia
- Impotence
- Knee issues
- Lung Problems
- Menopause
- Rheumatism
- Hands Trembling
- Stress

Balancing the Challenges of the Number 1

The first step in balancing the challenge is to feel free to say, " I need to ... ". When you feel intimidated by authoritarian, dogmatic, or fast people, speak up. You have the right to make your own decisions because your desires are worth as much as those of others. Remember to focus on your ambitions. It is possible that you lose supporters if your ideas are unconventional but take responsibility for yourself and move on. It may take unpleasant gestures or act when others choose to wait. You have to have the courage to try out your original ideas.

If you do not try, you will never go wrong. If you do a lot of things, the odds are you will not always hit the first time. But you will learn to decide, and this is what you need. You will feel good when you realize that you have control of your life. Forget the expectations of others, dare to be yourself, and recognize that, as pioneering, ingenious and independent individuals, "some of us have won, and some of us have lost."

Automotive

Youth:

As a child, the child feels a strong urge to stay together in their concrete world and a difficult period in their lives, of those who wish to explore. Maybe children do not usually make their own decisions, but the number one motivation often frustrates them when they are unable to follow their own instincts.

The solitary 1, determined, may find it difficult to adjust to the regimes adopted by troubled parents and become disobedient. Excessive restrictions may leave the child defeated, insecure, and powerless. Still, too much dependence on the child may generate fits of anger or inertia, if not tempered by the balance that stimulates individuality. Finally, for the parents, other authorities, and the child, the period before emotional and financial independence is particularly difficult.

Maturity:

Adult 1 wants to control his activities and rarely hears the advice of others. The 1 wants—although they do not need it—partners who support it. And as an accommodating loner, he plans accomplishments that, hopefully, attract praise and adeptness. In general, leader and manager, the number 1 prefer to leave the details to the subordinates or to another significant person. When personally or professionally involved with colleagues, he prides himself on his executive ability and easily embarrasses himself with the incompetence of the subordinates. When caught in personal error, the number 1 feels humiliated and takes immediate steps to keep up appearances

For these self-sufficient and cerebral individuals, love and marriage may not be primal motivation. Numbers 1 oscillate between introversion and companionship depending on their immediate goal. They may feel bold after realizing their ambitions and deciding that it is time to start a family. When they feel the need for self-glorification, they can decide to be the center of one's world without giving up their independence.

Balanced numbers 1 do not allow others to have them. They need to relate to supportive and diplomatic admirers, who obviously recognize (and applaud) their originality and achievements. The wedding of two motivations number 1 will base your attraction on activity and experimentation. There is little time for individual recognition. Since the number of self-motivation describes what we need to be comfortable, the partnership of two motivations number 1 will result in two convinced aspirants seeking adjustment on the other.

Self-Image

Youth:

Lying in bed, listening to music and wondering, "How will I be when I grow up? How will I walk, dress, and talk?" the number 1 preadolescents see themselves as future exclusive individuals. They dream of pioneering explorations of the Alps and find themselves flattered by being the first to reach the summit. Children with self-image number 1 imagine themselves as bosses, organizers, and inventors. They can be creative in supplying the dishwasher, or by redesigning the vacuum cleaner. They are always in a hurry—planning ambitious adventures, eager to reach the independence that maturity offers.

They always seem to stand to take the lead. They are more attracted by the instigations than by the detailed work, or the good finishes. They strive automatically to get others to work for them. Therefore, number 1, teenagers should be encouraged to see themselves performing tasks from start to finish and not just whipping others or promoting the end result.

Maturity:

Upon exiting an elevator, or entering a room-before the personality or intellect takes action, the adult number 1 emits vibrations of being different and of being in movement. Their attitude indicates strength, and they seem to transpire vitality.

Number 1 adults perceive themselves as commanding people. By living according to their self-image, the first impression they make implies strength, mastery, and self-affirmation. The number of self-expression can govern the first impression if career requirements, included in the meaning of the number, indicate uniforms, stylized functional dress codes or fashion.

Self-Expression

Youth:

Adults find it obvious when children have 1 as a self-expression number. The young number 1 believes in leadership and that some of their trusted followers will support their game. When they grow up, others will stick to them when the authorities choose them to hold leadership positions. Sometimes they may seem like tyrants, alienated, and discreet adults at the same time. The 1 are affirmative, instigating, and egoistic energy. It's hard for them to stand still for a long time, without boredom and innovative suggestions.

The number 1 talents take these kids to the director's chair. They will be more capable adults if they can develop in their own cadence and in their own way. Their creative ideas will immediately move the authorities. If praised, the inquisitive mind number 1 will elaborate on new projects.

Maturity:

Suggested Occupations: Inventor, designer, salesman, pilot, explorer, architect, buyer, seller, actor/actress, director, promoter, writer, publisher, conductor or musician, contractor, illustrator, cartoonist, politician, or any career that requires independent action, as well as a career that requires independent action, leadership and originality.

Destiny

This destiny indicates a life of self-development. To make the most of Numerology's farsightedness, Number 1 should never expect to depend on others. The individual may prefer to follow leaders in their youth. If one does, one is usually placed in subordinate positions until one becomes indispensable.

Personal Year

Year 1 is the first year of the nine-year cycle of experience and results in the challenge of qualification and performance based on your goals. It's time to shock conceptualized ideas three years earlier. For most, the people and experiences found this year promote rebirth. For the others, the year focuses on the promotion of new schemes and adds larger dimensions to current interests. Personal year number 1 allows the individual to tie, between January and August, the ends that remained loose in the previous year. The intensification of activity and the clarity of purpose this year increase in September—month number 1 in year number 1.

Change and independent thinking are key issues in this powerful year. This is no time to settle in or hesitate. The year begins slowly and provides the events with surprising twists and turns that in April, change the ideas. July offers the individual a chance to take control—to plan, build, and act. This act then establishes the stage of abandoning previous commitments in August. September's activities intensify new perspectives and the need for change. Between September 21 and 30, the individual must check the impracticalities and open the way to the new long-term ambitions.

Personal Month

The personal month number 1 of any personal year is operative, and the 1 must take the initiative. And the month in which the things that were about to be completed three months ago are carried out, but not materialized. Situations will arise this month that will put the individual in the driver's seat. New people, situations, and ideas abound. The 1 must be aggressive and use the period to make changes. Decisions should be based on independent and intellectual assessments since aid and encouragement should not be forthcoming. On the whole, the focus should be on beginnings.

Personal Day

Wake up with a determined attitude. Whether you are heading for a new job, a prospect, or any situation you want to promote, a smart new approach will open doors that have been closed. Extra-sensory perception is working, use intuition, stick to convictions, and do not lose control. The outlook will be new; therefore, grasp the opportunities that the day offers to be original.

You will be surprised to note that ambition, self-confidence, and creative thinking are all in the air, and you will feel satisfied today. Activate today's energetic and independent state of mind by wearing a tie or a red outfit. Above all, do not be lazy. Carefully plan all personal appointments and make sure you have a set goal. Stay tuned and use the practical evaluations to see your ideas complete. Because this working day has a purpose, it must be used decisively to begin something new.

Chapter 6: Number 2 – Cooperation

Attributes

Positive – Contributor, attentive, Diplomatic, Emotional, Compassionate, Responsive, Adaptable

Negative – Insensitive, pusillanimous, Impolite, Careless, critic, Shy, Fearful, disinterested, indifferent, Sly

Correspondents

LETTERS: B K, T

DISPOSAL: Concerned emotionally and personally

MENTAL AND PERSONAL ATTAINMENT NUMBERS:

11, 20, 29, 38, 47, 56, 65, 74, 83, 92, 101

COLOR: Orange

GEMA: Adultery

CRYSTAL: Rutile

VEGETATION: Eggs, Poultry, Sheep, Nuts

INSTRUMENTS/MUSICAL APPEAL: Zeal, Organ, Aria

MUSICAL NOTE: D (When tuned, C sharp)

PLANET: Moon

MONTHS: February and November (Shared with the number 11)

DAYS OF BIRTH: 2, 11, 20, 29 (11 and 29 are shared with the number 11)

DAY OF THE WEEK: Monday

NUMBERS GENERAL COMPATIBILITY: 2, 4, 6, 7 (8 in the business plan)

NUMBERS INCOMPATIBILITY: 5 (9, in commercial terms)

Note: If the individual has the number challenge 2, these descriptions will go from positive to negative until the challenge is balanced. Please be sure to read the meaning of the challenge.

Challenges of the Number 2

It is a challenge to the individual's sensitivity, perceptions, and susceptibility. It has a root in precocious attention too much or scarce with the feelings and the emotional reactions of the bearer of the challenge. The woman, generally the mother, either is very supportive and is too involved or is absent because of illness, divorce, or death. The father may have been very kind and receptive, and have played the role of the 'woman,' which may have unbalanced the child. Therefore, the baby becomes an adult without understanding whether to expect too much, too little or how much, indulging in intimate relationships.

It is difficult for children with challenging 2 to reach maturity by relying on themselves. They do not recognize their exclusivity, nor do they imagine living or working alone. These children are often indecisive because of the talent they have for seeing all the details on both sides of the same coin.

The No. 2 challenge users expect from themselves and their loved ones too much self-sacrifice. If the father or mother was a martyr, there is already a marked example that these children must overcome. As adults, the 2 always put themselves at the disposal of others. They back off and refuse to give up anything again. It is difficult for those in Challenge 2 to realize that they are not the only ones to have been bothered by sadness, loneliness, or malaise.

How do challenge 2 people abandon their defenses, break habits, and throw away misrepresented childhood impressions? First, they must remember that the universe does not revolve around themselves, their sensitivities, or their emotional relationships. Their defensiveness, surprisingly, establishes habits that put their personal feelings above the rights of others. Challenge number 2 can swing from one to the other of the following extremes until it is recognized and new habits that stabilize the sensitivity of the challenge bearer begin.

- Too sweet or too bitter.
- Very personal or very impersonal.
- Very open or very closed.
- Very grumpy or very grateful.
- Very humble (apologizes) or without remorse.
- Very helpless or very helpful.
- Very attentive or very rude. Very honest or with two faces.
- Very clement or very evil.
- Very hurt or too hard.
- Very dependent or very lonely.
- Very soft or very rough.
- Very friendly or very cold.
- Very unhappy or very loving.

Physical Challenges of the Number 2

A person's attitude sends a message to the brain that tells the body to scream for help. In order to attract attention to their malaise, people usually get sick or form negative habits. Numerologists believe that illness and well-being depend on attitude, and challenges indicate attitudes that result from feelings of need. When we do not feel needy, we feel good, balanced, and do not beg the attention of others. Essentially, if the personality challenges are balanced, the body's chemistry will also be balanced, and therefore, the likelihood of mental or physical illness will be small.

Challenge numbers indicate the ways in which people punish themselves for not being consciously generous to themselves.

The list of diseases and negative habits below relates to the challenge of number 2.

- Athlete's Foot
- Multiple Sclerosis
- Birth Defects
- Early Burns Leg Syndrome
- Restless
- Circulatory Problems
- Sciatica
- Diabetes
- Problems of Throat
- Fevers
- Tonsillitis
- Foot Problems

- Tuberculosis
- Hair Loss
- Urinary Tract Infections
- Hepatic Stains
- Vaginitis
- Menopause Problems

Balancing the Challenges of the Number 2

The first step in balancing the challenge is to feel free to say, "I need kindness." Ignore the insults and pessimism of the past. Forgive and forget. Always expect the best. Use a gentle way of asserting yourself without going to the extreme of prefacing every request with numerous and exaggerated greetings. If you are aware of yourself, remember that others want to know what you think of them. We all seek approval; therefore, stop criticizing. The reflector is not always aimed at you.

When you're out of time for yourself because you're a slave to others, remember that supporting, sharing, and collaborating does not mean losing your identity. It's admirable to be a part of an effort, but you do not have to take care of every detail, nor treat everyone with fur gloves. Be peaceful, but not at the expense of your sanity. Be yourself and recognize that, like adaptive, caring, and supportive individuals, you do not have to depend on others to make decisions, for your peace of mind or self-esteem.

Automotive

Youth:

As a baby, the yearning that the number 2 child feels are to be at peace, to be friendly and happy. When rebuked, this child is bored more than expected. The disharmony, of any kind, can cause the individual to almost cry. When the child is surrounded by questioning authorities, as non-sympathetic brothers, and is the target of unjust criticism, his school and social behavior will suffer. The young number 2 wants to give and receive love, care, and consideration. For parents, a number 2 child can be "gentle, placid and affable." These are words that describe the individual when surrounded by flexible, soft, and patient authorities.

The young number 2 wants to be appreciated for the little things he does. A supportive position, from which you can be prudent, courteous, and diplomatic, will leave you at ease. The individual can warm up with the reflected glory of leaders and authorities, for example, and is adaptable and tolerant when involved in group activities. Still, music and rhythm are in your soul, and dance and music lessons—zeal or horn—can prepare you to associate with equals in cooperative adventures in which you can shine.

Maturity:

2 adults want friends, unpretentious love, and comfort. Surround yourself with people who need them because they prefer to do things for others. Rigorous schedules, strict orders, and demanding authorities cause them discomfort. These individuals like to exchange confidences with close friends. The 2 are confident—quiet, helpful, hear the problems.

Aggressive (and corrosive) friends, employers, and companions are attracted to self-motivating people number 2 because the modest 2 do not constitute a threat to leadership, position, and power ambitions. The 2 do not object to forming a support system for more affirmative and dominant friends and colleagues. In their subtle form, the two can impose their points of view. They get what they want and attract recognition for being the amalgam of marriages, families, and business.

The balanced 2 divide or receive credit and recognition with humility. They are, in general, very grateful to small favors, and are pleased to reciprocate. Controlling leaders, however, can intimidate them. In the effort to meet demands, they can exhaust their energy. The 2 are well able to deny themselves for the benefit of others.

Self-Image

Youth:

When lying in bed, listening to music and imagining, "How will I be when I grow up? How do I walk, dress and talk? " The preadolescent number 2 sees himself as a supportive individual. He dreams of a perfect marriage in which, without ties, he helps his partner, and the couple, nestled in a peaceful atmosphere, cautiously climbs the ladder towards comfort and happiness. The number 2 is seen well-maintained, safe, and cozy.

Children with self-image number two find themselves partners, group leaders, and diplomats. They can solve domestic disputes between siblings and parents can learn to sew or iron and get delighted with little treasures that accumulate and grow.

Maturity:

Upon leaving the elevator or entering a room—before the intellect or personality take action—adults number 2 emit prudent and unpretentious vibrations. Their attitude indicates courtesy, and they have a refined and paced look. They tend to subjugate themselves to dress fashions and neutral tones. In order not to be individualistic, the 2 are noted for their elegance and their care with details and accessories.

Self-Expression

Youth:

Adults find it obvious when a child has self-expression number 2. In youth, the number 2 talents are based on the ability to support. The young follow the leader during the jokes. As they grow older, they find that they do not feel comfortable attracting attention. They may decline to make suggestions and be intimidated in the situations that make them stand out.

When teens or young adults, the 2 are good students, they have the talent to be diplomatic, detailed, and skillful organizers. Dance and music classes are good exits for their artistic skills, and group activities provide them with comfortable recognition. These supportive young people will relate their talents to the instigations, leadership, and creative ideas of family, friends, and authorities.

Maturity:

Suggested Occupations: Secretary, professor, diplomat, accounting technician, accountant, librarian, statistician, biographer, bacteriologist, politician, civil servant, poet, columnist, technical writer, novelist, editor, group singer, group dancer, musician, etc.

The number 2 talents must recognize their own need and desire for harmony and time to perform their tasks carefully. In a work environment, they should set aside emotional judgments and not allow sensitive reactions to color their attitudes. The 2s are concerned about the opinion of others. Balanced number 2 talents prefer to team up with partners and engage in jobs where minutiae are essential, as well as gentle persuasion rather than command. Generally friendly, quiet, and reserved at work, these individuals may choose roles that allow them to interact, one at a time, with individual executives and/or groups.

Destiny:

For this number, achieving harmony is the ultimate goal. Attaining balance is important in order to allow a fulfilling life. It is important to strike a balance between both negative and positive traits. While there is nothing wrong with focusing primarily on positive traits, no one is ever perfect. So, using positive traits to offset the negative as much as possible. Once balance is achieved, number 2's find a happy and fulfilling life.

Personal Year

Year 2 is the second year of the nine-year cycle of experience and results in the accuracy and qualification of performance based on the goals set in the first year. It is time to let the experiences recently instigated in the previous year solidify. During the personal year number 2, it is possible to discover who the true friends are and how to be a true friend to others. It's better to play the Mona Lisa and smile mysteriously than to let the little annoyances cause more divisions.

Money comes to the hills, small problems come to fruition, and delays can irritate. Personal year number 2 is an occasion to observe, refine, and be willing to take on the responsibility of keeping the peace. Nothing new begins, but you need to maintain friendly relationships with the people who will be around for the next seven years.

Personal Month

The personal month number 2 in the personal year offers the opportunity to make others happy. Interactions with friends and lovers are a top priority, and ambitious material changes must be postponed. The previous month was laborious and tiring, and now it's time to rest and give your close friends time to digest and adjust to things that may be different from your personal desires. With an open mind, listen to insinuations and constructive criticisms that may be helpful: be kind, adaptable, and understanding in the face of events.

Personal Day

Wake up with a favorable attitude. Whether going to the office, for a day out or for the automatic washer, go slow, watching and feeling the weather. Use intuition when engaging with others. Responding responsively to the needs of others will keep things in peace. Be generous, understanding, and helpful. In return, expect to receive the assistance of family and co-workers today. Do not panic; the time is not propitious to force results.

Accept everything that happens today and has faith that there will be future benefits if you do not try to change plans or relationships. This day has a purpose: it must be used in support of yesterday's activities, to absorb information and reaffirm alliances.

Chapter 7: Number 3 – Communication

Attributes

Positive – Optimistic, imaginative, talented, sociable, Fun, Good Taste, happy, Talkative, Young, Friendly, Greedy

Negative – Disjointed, Complainant, Quirky, Superficial, Tattletale, Narcissistic, Defeated, Distanced, Liar, humdrum

Correspondents

LETTERS: C, L, U

NUMBERS: 12, 21, 30, 39, 48, 57, 66, 75, 84, 93, 102

COLOR: Yellow Yolk

CRYSTAL: Topaz, Galena

VEGETATION: Narcissus-Of-Meadows, Honeysuckle, Orchid, Pink, Pansy, Elm, Mahogany, Sequoia Sempervirens

FOOD: Romaine, Duck, Potato, Tomato, Pudding, Grapes

INSTRUMENTS/PLEA MUSICAL: Bugle, Trombone, Band

MUSICAL NOTE: Mi (When tuning: F)

PLANET: Venus

MONTHS: March to December

DAYS OF BIRTH: 3, 12, 21, 30

DAY OF WEEK: Wednesday

NUMBER OF GENERAL COMPATIBILITIES: 1, 3, 5, 6 (9, business plan)

INCOMPATIBILITY NUMBERS: 4, 7 (8, commercial)

Challenges of the Number 3

This is a challenge to the individual's communication skills, imagination, and sociability. In particular, the mother and siblings together, or the grandmother and the mother as a whole, either made a lot of fun of the child or put him to bed. The young number 3 is often an only child, boy or girl, the eldest or the youngest in the family. As the preferred or neglected child, challenge 3 becomes a self-aware adult on the social plane, not understanding what he or she has for others. He is incapable of seeing beyond superficial judgments and maturing elegantly.

Challenge number 3 can provide superior talent for warmth, humor, artistic expression, and optimism, or the tendency to be intolerant, cynical, spendthrift, or pessimistic. Be that as it may, the 3 are born communicators, they can light a room when they express joy or cause everyone to feel uneasy when they experience sadness. When teens, the 3 or make real scandals with the fall of a hat, or they remain silent. They are extravagant, whether they be heroes or losers. Married, they are jealous or indifferent. When the problems caused by their jealousy become very painful, the 3 simulate alienation. As adults, the 3 perceive friendship as the key that opens the door to love—or else they never reveal themselves or make any commitment to build an alliance. They trust too much—they accept words, gestures, and people without feeling the underlying factors—or, suspiciously, refuse to accept anything by appearance.

Physical Challenges of the Number 3:

This number is with specific physical ailments mainly associated to the upper back and shoulders. These ailments generally come in the form of pain an discomfort as a result of "shouldering the burden". Here are some other physical ailments which may affect number 3s:

- Upper back pain
- Shoulder discomfort

- Neck stiffness
- Migraines
- Sore throat (prone to infection)
- Eyesight (sharpness deteriorating over time)
- Bad posture (especially in taller individuals)

Balancing the challenges of the Number 3

Number 3s are characterized by being sensitive. This is why having outlets that can help 3s manage their feelings is essential. These can come in the way of sports or arts. It really doesn't matter what type of outlet it is so long as it allows 3s to express their feelings in such a way that it becomes constructive rather than destructive.

Also, physical ailments can be improved by allowing 3s to let their feelings out, either by being able to talk about them or simply express them creatively. In addition, 3s are sensitive to the pain of others. So, don't be surprised if you, as a 3, end up feeling discomfort as a result of the empathy you have developed for another person.

Self-Image

Youth:

The talents of number 3 are based on cordiality, imagination, and artistic penchant. As they grow older, the number 3 learns they can talk, dramatize, and pound to get rid of either the practical work or the related responsibilities. When frustrated, they may seem very spoiled, foolish, or theatrical. As charming, customizable, trustworthy little critters, it is difficult for them to suppress their imagination or to stall the chatter.

Without wishing to lie, dramatic number 3 can alter the facts, imitate, or make a scene. 3 strive to be attractive or more interesting. The talents of number 3 place the child in the light of the reflectors. As an adult, they will have a more fertile mind, be more educated, and have a better taste if they are encouraged to verbalize, paint, play an instrument, dance, or write.

Maturity:

Suggested Occupations: Writing—and all means of self-expression that focus on the word. Master of ceremonies, model, actor, designer, artist, musician, singer, salesman, decorator, lecturer, dressmaker, jeweler, social secretary, buyer, bookseller, telephonist, gift wrapper, evangelist, account executive, event promoter, defense or prosecution lawyer, pharmacist, cartoonist, comedian, etc.

Self-Expression

Youth:

Communication is a challenge for 3s when they are young. They may have some trouble with being able to express themselves effectively though they may attempt to express it in other ways. As a result, young 3s will endeavor in any number of creative and artistic tasks. If care is taken to foster these talents, older 3s will have no trouble handling their communication skills and thereby expressing their emotions. If left unattended, younger 3s will have a hard time relating to others. These are individuals who might be termed as having "little emotional intelligence".

Maturity:

As 3s get older, their communication skills become paramount to being able to express their feelings and ideas. This is very important as 3s who cannot fully express themselves will find it virtually impossible to connect with others simply because they are unable to relate with others on a more personal level. This may lead to trouble forming deeper and more meaningful relationships. Communicative 3s are able to provide tremendous insight and offer words of wisdom whenever required.

Destiny:

Number 3s are meant to be communicators by nature. When 3s develop their communication skills, they are able to let their skills shine through in their interactions with others. 3s are very competent journalists and writers. They might also enter other fields, such as counseling or social work. In short, any type of job or profession which involves communicating with others is right up number 3's alley.

Personal Year

The number 3 is the third year in the nine-year cycle of experience and results in the accuracy and qualification of performance based on the goals set in the first year. It is time to see the ideas and instigations that began two years ago, come to fruition. For most, it's a welcome change from the petty problems, the delays, and emotional worries of the previous year. It is the year that offers opportunities to enjoy lighter interests and increase social contacts. The personal year 3 requires attention to fashions, novelties, and fantasies. Buy clothes. Decorate your home a little. Create an atmosphere that attracts fun.

Love and happiness come to meet them and to bind them. Telephone and postal contacts should be the focus of activating social and business opportunities along with a year to ease workloads, give yourself time to play and take a vacation. Festivals, artistic skills, and lovely people should be the focus. Friends provide access to business, fun, and gifts.

Almost every month is lively except April and August. Old and new relationships should be encouraged. It may be that until October, there are only talks, but the topics discussed will bring functional and material goods the following year. For people with destination 3, this year's opportunities will be unforgettable. They should, however, keep the main goals in mind and avoid wasting time and money by exploring and expanding the avenues of self-expression. It's a year of pleasure. The romance can sprout and should be seen with a youthful touch. Colleagues may need to be listened to.

During personal year number 3, contacts will be made that provide social activity or attract responses to creative engagements. Work year number 4, below, will not be focused on activities that are impractical or less constructive. This year has a purpose—to relieve tensions and worries. It provides time to watch the amusements promoted by others and to discover creative methods. The year revisits the interest and understanding of the possible joys of feeling in relationships with other people. It sows humor and reminds us that life can be beautiful.

Personal Month

Personal month number 3 in any personal year gives the individual the opportunity to feel unconcerned, lively, and self-expressive. Joyful companions, parties, and all forms of communication are important now. This is no time to pout and stay indoors. After the brakes of the previous month, enjoy this to get out, be seen and heard. The projects started two months ago will now flourish. It's time to tell others about them. Situations will arise that require attractive appearance and happy physiognomy. Look for old friends. Make a note of someone's phone number at a party and be sure to call to make a new account. Buy clothes and decorative items for the home. Be prepared to entertain and be entertained. Use this month to verbalize ideas, display talents, and have fun interacting with friends and loved ones.

Personal Day

Wake up with a happy, lively, and friendly attitude. Whether going to the office, for a day out, or for the automatic washer, chant a melodious song on the way. Invite a friend over for dinner or wait to be invited. Make this day cheerful and keep an upbeat attitude. Work can seem like a joke and, if that's the case, your mental picture will be contagious. Spread the good news or a joke and dress yourself to attract attention. Hold onto the fun and give others the pleasure of your company.

You may see a lot of talks and little action. This is the day that sets the stage for tomorrow's self-discipline and practical approach. Use this day to make someone smile. Do not let fatalists and those who spread sorrows crush anyone's spirit.

Now there is time for hobbies and conversations. Go to the theatre. Play with children and pets. Curl up with a humorous lover and enjoy a good laugh. Loosen up the routines and relax the material goals. Take the initiative to pick up the phone and make time to listen and respond. Above all, go for the sun, and avoid talking about personal problems and anxieties.

Savor what comes today with a pinch of salt and realize that what may seem too worried is a superficial thing, it will not come true. Certain conversations will involve projects that require practical planning opportunities in the future. This busy day should be used to relax, play, and exchange ideas with positive thinkers.

Chapter 8: Number 4 – Practicality

Attributes

Positive – Practical, Disciplined, Loyal, Organized, Ordered, Factual, Franco, Constructive, Cautious.

Negative – Unproductive, Incompetent, Negligent, Inflexible, Careless, Coarse, Miserly, Rigid.

Correspondents

LETTERS: D, M, V

NUMBERS: 13, 22, 31, 40, 49, 58, 67, 76, 85, 94, 103

COLOR: Green

GEMS: Emerald, Green Jade

CRYSTAL: Cassiterite

VEGETATION: Pepper, Pepper, Pod

FOOD: Grapefruit, Oysters, Veal, Ham, Cod, Yam, Carrot, Pie Morangas, Strawberries, Pretzels, Honey, Coffee.

INSTRUMENTS/MUSICAL APPEAL: Violin, Guitar, Lute; Instrumental.

MUSICAL NOTE: F sharp

PLANET: Saturn

MONTH: April

DAYS OF BIRTH: 4, 13, 22, 31

DAY OF THE WEEK: Thursday

NUMBERS OF GENERAL COMPATIBILITY: 2, 6, 8

INCOMPATIBILITY NUMBERS: 3, 5, 7, 9

Note: If the subject has challenge number 4, these descriptions go from positive to negative until the challenge is balanced. Make sure you read the meaning of the challenge.

Challenges of the Number 4

This is a challenge to the individual's attention to traditions, organizational skills, and the understanding of practical realities. The child often lacked contact with people who were attentive to their needs. Parents strove to provide the child with routine, exteriorities, and appropriate parenting—or else the child's environment lacked conventional planning, practical needs, and stability. Consequently, the child becomes an extremely organized, self-disciplined, and conservative adult—or else slow to work, careless, and unchanging.

The child may have learned to go to the bathroom with a whip. Schedules and specificities were detailed by the authorities even before the 4 had the emotional or physical ability to meet those requirements. Or the number 4 may not have repeated many routines, and authorities may not have expected great accomplishments or instilled in it the importance of meeting schedules. Either extreme causes frustration in the child and leads him to seek ways to plan and structure the future. The child either develops preventive methods and controls or else abhors the systems.

As adults, the 4 often focus too much on the details and the system. They plan and schematize everything and find it difficult to produce something without maximum dedication. Parents of 4, when working, given the need to match children and work, often choose parochial or military schools for ideal secondary learning. If these children are individualistic, creative, and imaginative, these rigid educational systems could make them feel fish out of water. On the contrary, if they are spared the quince stick and disciplinary standards, they may not learn that leadership and art also require concentration and discipline. For those with challenge 4 or there are too many rules or shortages, which limits their ability to be flexible or inflexible when there is a practical need to do so.

Challenge number 4 can swing from one to the other of the following extremes until the behavior of the challenge bearer is recognized, and new habits have initiated that update their practical self-assessments.

- Very disciplined or very sly.
- Very austere or very informal.
- Very effective or very limited.
- Very practical or very impractical.
- Very economical or very wasteful.
- Very managerial or very unprepared.
- Very perfectionist or very careless.
- Too stiff or too loose.
- Very puritanical or very malicious.
- Very stubborn or very flexible.
- Very ritualistic or very random.
- Too lazy or too busy.
- Very intolerant of very open. Very repressed or very free.

Physical Challenges of the Number 4

This list of illnesses and negative habits relates to the challenge of number 4.

- Hypoglycemia

- Blood Problems
- Insomnia
- Vehicle Sickness
- Jaundice
- Cataract
- Liver Problems
- Cystitis
- Migraines
- Foot Puncture
- Rickets
- Gastrointestinal Problems
- Genital Herpes
- Dental Problems
- Halitosis
- Sucking Fingers

Balancing the Challenges of the number 4

The first step in balancing the challenge is to feel free to say, "I need security." Ignore any approach too serious or too free. Use only the restrictions that make it possible for you to live today, and when planning, imagine that you will live 1,000 years. It's your choice. Listen to your feelings. Embrace a friend. Try to relax—who knows!

Dedicate yourself to a sensitive workload and schedule. Work five days a week and save the weekends for fun. Make commitments, make a daily agenda, and control the trade and social constraints. You can maintain a slow but steady lifestyle that will give you long-term security. Spend money on necessities and save for the pleasures.

Automotive

Youth:

When reprimanded, they will try to find the rule or routine that will give them back firmness. These babies need direct instruction and discipline. The young number 4 are conformed, conscientious, and serious. When surrounded by disorganized authorities, they will be negligent or stubborn. Parents can describe child number 4 as trustworthy, determined and methodical, words that describe the individual when surrounded by controlled, sober, and trustworthy authorities.

The four have a legitimate interest in preserving conventions and traditions. As they are very decorous, exaggerated displays of love and intimacy may not appeal to them. They love respect, regularity, and unpretentiousness. Family, community, and national pride win loyalty. However, too much self-discipline can be problematic at maturity if these children do not receive affection and affection.

Maturity:

The number 4 adults want to be deliberate, efficient, and trustworthy. They need to structure and steer tasks or goals diligently and feel safe, constant, and convenient. This posture seems somewhat inflexible and resistant to novelties, and it is. They are capable of intense self-sacrifice and feel that without the principles of commitment, stability is an impossible dream.

The number 4 people do not like to be rude or mischievous. Rarely ill-educated or rude friends and lovers need to know what is expected of them in order to satisfy the desires of others. The 4 must receive outlined tasks, and every trustworthy convention, every leader they can rely on, and every practical tool will command their attention. The 4 want material goals and feel more comfortable with people who work to meet traditional needs and help them plan the future. One problem with self-motivation number 4 is the fear of changing routines. They think that loosening them will cause confusion, problems, and loss of control.

Self-Image

Youth:

Lying in bed, listening to music, and thinking, "How will I be when I grow up?" The number 4 is seen as a safe citizen. They dream of leading orderly, respected, and savored lives. The boys see themselves as national protectors, receiving from the country the highest honors for the fulfillment of duty. The girls find themselves diligent owners of a white house with green lawn, well-protected with the traditional fence of pointy stakes. Children with self-image number 4 see themselves as diligent, dignified, and orderly.

When young, the 4 do not care about trends, news, or fleeting fashions. When surrounded by vivacious and enthusiastic equals, they may seem slow or demanding. Their dream is to control the people and the situations they encounter, because people who are susceptible to be instigated do not make them comfortable, and dodge when they are hurried or undecided. Self-Image number 4 indicates a sturdy body and majestic presence.

Maturity:

As they step out of the elevator or into a room—before the personality or intellect comes into action—the number 4 adults emit carefully upright and conservative vibrations. Their attitude indicates personality with business characteristics, and they seem controlled and attentive. The first impression they give is dependable and sometimes rustic.

Adults that are number 4 become administrators. When they live according to self-image, the first impression implies a failure to solve practical problems. The number of self-expression can govern the first impression as long as formal, fleeting, or extravagant dress codes are indicated in the functional descriptions of the meaning of the number. However, when the 4 live according to the self-image, they do not display the corresponding colors indicated by a number in another part of their numerological map.

Self-Expression

Youth:

As they grow up, the 4 discover that they can follow instructions, prepare for activities, and fabricate or fix things to be recognized. When frustrated, they can be servile, insensitive, and resist routines. These helpful, thoughtful, serious, and methodical people feel happier when they contribute to a family project. It is difficult not to be stunned by the unyielding practical energy of the 4.

When teens or young adults, the 4 conserve established a routine and focus on things that require personal attention to detail. These teens are not social butterflies or intellectual magicians. They are planners, maintainers, and natural producers of useful products or materials. The 4 need and go to work to obtain material goods. Carpentry, auto mechanics, embroidery, and sewing can keep them occupied. They are not idle and will study, play some sport or find work after school.

Maturity:

As number 4s reach maturity, their logical and organized nature makes the ideal planners. They are the kind of folks who are methodical and need to figure everything out before the endeavor into any kind of activity. In some extreme cases, this may lead to inaction because they are chronically hesitant about carrying something out. In the best of cases, they have the foresight and the vision to conduct some of the biggest and most ambitious projects.

Destiny

Since 4s are great at planning, carrying out structured projects and following instructions, any kind of job such as construction, development and even real estate brokerage are ideal professions. Also, ambitious endeavors that require a great deal of thought and careful attention to detail may suit 4s well. Project engineers, software developers and researchers are often very competent number 4s.

Personal Year

The number 4 is the fourth in the nine-year cycle of experiences and results in the hassle and qualification of performance based on the goals set in the first year. It's time to work and let the variety of interests and friendships of the previous year bring social activity. For most, this is a year-to-year to correct material mistakes made in the last three years. For others, the year focuses on giving and receiving orders, on doubling impulsiveness and paying attention to a basic routine and a work schedule. And a year of persevering, saving, and accumulating assets. The projects started three years ago.

Self-discipline, restraint, and endurance will be required to make the most of the options open this year. Careful planning, awareness, and efficient attitude are fundamental needs after the dispersion of the previous year. Keywords for this year are caution, dignity, and order. People who volunteer for growth partners this year are not creative, romantic, or open-minded. They are creeping, practical, do not like apathy, incompetence, or frivolity. Faith and trust will have their rewards, and dedication to work will, in addition, attract solidarity. And a year to be sound and rational, so as to correct misconceptions and cultivate long-term goals.

It is necessary to abstain from holidays, festive times, and unscheduled expenses. And you must be attentive to future gratifications. This is the year to buy a new home, repair the old house's roof or invest in another property. To make the most of this year, you need to be patient, serene, and practical. The methodical approach to day-to-day details and appointments is a must. Do not allow yourself to be constrained by physical responsibilities and demands. Identify the opportunities to put your subjects and your body in functional order. For example, get ready to take advantage of holidays, sexual pleasures, and chance to break the routine, which is offered the following year in personal year number 5. Get ready to savor freedom, change, and adventure, economizing and acting constructively at this time.

Personal Month

Personal month number 4 in any personal year gives the individual the opportunity to produce tangible results. Serious dedication to economics, routines, and physical fitness should be a top priority. Laziness, disorganization, and impracticality must be pushed back. The previous month did not include responsibilities, and there was time for friends, but now it's time to rebuild plans and projects, as well as set financial and judgmental mistakes. Situations that require a direct approach may arise. Use the occasion to be realistic.

Personal Day

Wake up early and organize plans with a determined attitude. Re-evaluate the details and get rid of mundane tasks. Control the impulses and keep the schedules. Be true to your goals. Use patience, perseverance, and judicious judgment to put the house, work, and social obligations in order. Do not be innovative or mutant. Follow the procedures, count on yourself, and retain dignity. This is no time to experiment or be lazy. Plans for tomorrow, made today, are likely to be changed or canceled, so deal with the details that might restrict the freedoms of tomorrow.

Make a personal commitment to persevere until things are done. Let the momentary needs guide the acts of today. Use sweat and planning and do what needs to be done to maintain conventions, discipline, and durability. Be frank and obedient in dealing with superiors; keep your composure, and be reasonable.

Chapter 9: Number 5 – Sexual Freedom

Attributes

Positive – Entrepreneur, Enthusiastic, Operative, Versatile, Intelligent, Lover of Freedom, Fertile, Sensual, Adventurous.

Negative – Irresponsible, Impetuous, Disapproved, Forgotten, Very sexualized, Not objective, Very indulgent, Monotonous, Old-fashioned

Correspondents

LYRICS: E, N, W

DISPOSITION: Sensual, Spontaneous, Inconvenient

NUMBERS: 14, 23, 41, 50, 59, 68, 77, 86, 95, 104

COLOR: Turquoise

GEM: Turquoise Aquamarine

CRYSTALS: white mica, hornblende

VEGETATION: carnation, gardenia, spring

FOODS: Lettuce, celery, cucumber, endive, beets, broccoli, apple, Cherry, Raspberry, Melon

INSTRUMENTS: Bells, Trumpet, Viola

MUSICAL NOTE: SOL (when challenged, G)

PLANET: Mars

MONTH: May

DAYS BIRTH: 5, 14, 23

DAY OF THE WEEK: Tuesday

GENERAL COMPATIBILITY NUMBERS: 1, 3, 7, 9

INCOMPATIBILITY NUMBERS: 2, 4, 6 (8, commercial)

Note: If an individual has the challenge of number 5, these descriptions will range from positive to negative until the challenge is balanced. Please be sure to read the meaning of the number of the code.

Challenges of the Number 5

It is a challenge to the individual's understanding of the physical aspects of life. It deals with freedom, of indifference, and of sexuality. As children, those facing the challenge are exposed to too much or too little loyalty. They do not learn when to join or when to change. Very confusing experiences tax the baby's adaptability, or else it is the adult's caution that binds them too much. This challenge is centered on the expectations that the users have of pleasure and pain, which have been influenced by too much curiosity or insufficient questions.

The number 5 challenge is attracted to sensitive, traditional, and obviously dependable people—or vice versa. They think that everyone who is different from them is interesting. Relationships are usually fleeting, or they drag painfully, and as soon as they understand a person or situation, they tend to be bored. Because of a confused sense of loyalty, the challenged are content to be dispassionate, or, then, enthusiastically discover a new interest.

As children, they may have witnessed very quick decision-making. As adults, they risk guesses, or else they investigate carefully before joining a new situation. It is difficult for the challenged to feel who is worthy of their devotion. Your intuitive talent for knowing when to change or what to change has been atrophied. Although immediate diagnosticians of others, the No. 5 challenge cannot spontaneously do what is right for themselves.

Challenge 5 can swing from one to the other of the following extremes until the behavior of the challenge bearer is recognized and new habits that stabilize his or her idleness, curiosity, and sensuality begin.

- Very free or very chained.
- Very versatile or very maladaptive.
- Very satisfied or very unhappy.
- Very irresponsible, or very careful.
- Very understanding or very evil.
- Very excitable or very calm.
- Very adaptable or very firm.
- Very curious or very inert.
- Very smart or very slow.
- Very loyal or very fickle.
- Very sensual or very cerebral.
- Too busy or too bored.
- Very impatient or very serene.
- Very lucky or very unlucky.

Physical Challenges of the Number 5

This list of negative illnesses and habits relates to the challenge of number 5.

- Abortions
- Gum Problems
- Abscesses
- Hemorrhoids
- Accidents
- Infections
- Acne
- Anxiety Problems
- Arthritis
- Multiple Sclerosis
- Brain Tumor
- Obesity

Balancing The Challenge Of Number 5

The first step in balancing the challenge is to feel free to say, "I need to be free." Hold on to a materially productive purpose. Forget the inconsistencies or the unconvincing disappointments of childhood and remember that you are adaptable. Use the mind to observe, learn, and explore. Stick to a person or job until you get to the details and gain experience. Show your enthusiasm to less curious souls because you have the ability to be a catalyst for change in the lives of others. See people from other angles, stimulate new relationships, and let them evolve.

See yourself an enthusiastic wildflower, versatile and adaptable, while recognizing that your attitude can make you feel like a weed. But always remember that a weed is a flower that is in the wrong place. Cate carefully your flower beds!

Automotive

Youth:

As a child, the number 5 momentum these children feel is that they are curious, active, and free from restraints. When reprimanded, they become bored or moody. Children number 5 need to apply their enthusiasm and energy in a stimulating way mentally and physically. These young people are discontented, impatient and daring. Therefore, when surrounded by pragmatic authorities, fixed in routine and solemn, they will be unpredictable or wild. The 5 want progressive, imaginative, and open-minded leadership.

Sports, student politics, journalism, science, and the arts, in the mind of teenager number 5, can today occupy the first place, and tomorrow, the second. A member of the opposite sex can be your rival if you aim for supremacy by using other interests. The 5th may be the male or the sexual muse of the class. An adventure on horseback, on a motorcycle, or challenging the great open space can increase your reserve of life experiences. 5 has a continual impulse to move from some fascinating unknown to another, and rarely relaxes its need for expansion.

Maturity:

Adults 5 want to stay young, thought-provoking, and moving. The 5 are entrepreneurs who need to find exits to their curiosity and use their enthusiasm to inspire others to experience unfamiliar directions or to probe the depths. They want to feel unimpeded, free of responsibility, with an open mind, and a little inconvenience. If this seems unconventional, it is, just as they are. The 5 are often catalysts for changes in the lives of others. They try everything that is new to themselves and take advantage of speculation.

One problem with self-motivation number 5 is the fear of being tied up. They think that if they settle conventionally, their style will be atrophied. Business, social, intimate, and family relationships must adapt to their rapid cadence and mutant ideas. Over time, various people and experiences excite their fantasy. They retain anything or anyone that cannot be assimilated or schematized and easily forget the unpleasant experiences. The balanced 5 live the now.

Self-Image

Youth:

Lying in bed, listening to music, and thinking, "How will I be when I grow up? How am I going to walk, dress, and talk?" Young numbers 5 look like deranged demons. They dream of leading a life without hindrance, of discoveries at random and unconventional. The boys see themselves winning the biggest lottery prize in the country and spending it all on pleasures. Girls find themselves traveling the world, meeting mythical people and directing attention to wherever it takes them the pleasure of wandering. Self-image children can see themselves as uninhibited adventurers, fearless, and provocative sex symbols.

Young people whose dreams are based on the meaning of number 5 can be too adventurous and create confusion. They affirm themselves to have freedom of choice and action. Their joint aspect is out of the ordinary: they are to stop the traffic.

Maturity:

When exiting the elevator or entering a room—before personality or intellect comes into action—the adult number 5 emits provocative, non-traditional, and sociable vibration. His attitude indicates a vibrant personality and seems willing to everything. The first impression she gives is energetic, sometimes lively, and always determined. If self-expression and self-expression numbers are introverted or conventional, the 5 look well-groomed and colorful. Dress styles, posture, and attitude do not necessarily indicate their sensual or adventurous self-image.

Self-Expression

Youth:

When they grow up, the 5 do not follow instructions, do not stand still, or accept rigid routines. To dodge problems, they seduce disciplinarians and teachers. They are helping people, fertile in solutions and gossip, are always eager to add enthusiasm to family projects. It's hard not to be surprised by their intelligence, inventiveness, and adaptability.

Maturity:

A mature 5 is all about achieving ultimate self-expression. From the experience that they have accumulated over the years, they are able to better express their wishes and desires. They allow them to have a greater degree of freedom and liberation. They are able to embrace who they are and make the most of the time that is ahead of them. Many 5s have gotten a grip on their sexuality regardless of what their orientation might be. They have reached a point in their lives where they are comfortable with being who they are.

However, 5s who have not come to grips with who they are will struggle to find a balance in their later years. These may lead to feelings of bitterness and resentment, particularly if they feel sexually unsatisfied. It is important to note that they may find other ways of liberating this type of pent up energy though they may still feel frustrated or unfulfilled to a certain extent.

Destiny

5s tend to be extroverted and outgoing. They enjoy being the spotlight and in contact with people. They are great at getting along with other people. The service industry is the first stop for 5s. Here are some suggested pccupations: Actor, lecturer, writer, theatrical producer, promoter of events, advertising, street vendor, public relations specialist, reservations agent, politician, advertising consultant, lawyer, psychologist, director of personnel, engineer-designer, inventor investigator, detective, insurance inspector, newspaper reporter, among others.

Personal Year

The number 5 is the fifth in the nine-year cycle of experience that results in the accuracy and qualification of performance based on the goals set in the first year. It's time to get away from the routines, keeping in mind the practical assessments of the previous year when it may come with sexual pleasures and transitions. For the most part, it is a time of rapid cadence—filled with people and new scenarios—aimed at sowing curiosity, adding versatility, resulting in a broader perspective. For the others, the year focuses on accommodating an indoctrination that began in October of the previous year. It's an energetic year to learn from experience, discard old ideas, and think about seeing long-term goals from a different angle. It is necessary to keep in mind the material ambitions in risking a new approach to business, home, and lifestyle.

You have to risk the unknowns and not be afraid to make spontaneous decisions. It is not a year to buy a home or assume new responsibilities. To make the most of this year, we must relieve the obligations of daily work and eliminate practical and emotional hindrances. The voluntary, vigorous, and original approach to the many possibilities offered should make this a lively year.

Year 5 will test the individual's ability to feel free, at ease, and yet remain constructive. Understand that progress depends on tolerance and taking advantage of new experiences and does not anticipate the end result or prejudge how people will interact. The attitude is very significant: it is better to swim in favor of the tide.

Personal Month

Personal month number 5 in any one year personal provides the opportunity to make transitions and changes. Extravagant ideas, travel, and the drive to reduce responsibility should have top priority. Narrow views, stiffness, and continued efforts should be put aside. The previous month was filled with realities and practical limitations, and there was little time for experimentation. Now is the time to risk love and luck. Enjoy the excitement, the new people, and the opportunities that open up. Situations may arise that require a premonition. Use this month to be an entrepreneur: try something different, something that attracts attention, and be spontaneous. Be flexible, enterprising, and keep your mind open when faced with unexpected possibilities.

Personal Day

Wake up sooner or later and openly address the unconventional opportunities of every hour. Whether going to the office, for a day off, or to the grocery store, do it differently. Try and change perspectives. Dress to stop the traffic, delay in lunch, and welcome with enthusiasm everything that comes. Be responsible when necessary, but allow yourself to feel indoctrinated, sociable, and sensual. In other words, expect to be flexible. Show everyone that you are the one that is indicated for the yaws, ready to take the direction at the time of change or change of plans.

Make a personal decision to do something that the moment instigates. Use the charm, the insight, and the adventurous ideas to disconcert someone, but make room for unprogrammed socialization or chance. Turn to the greater responsibilities of tomorrow, to the conventional obligations and to the priority of emotional relationships, living to regain routines and to make room for commitments.

Chapter 10: Number 6 – Formation

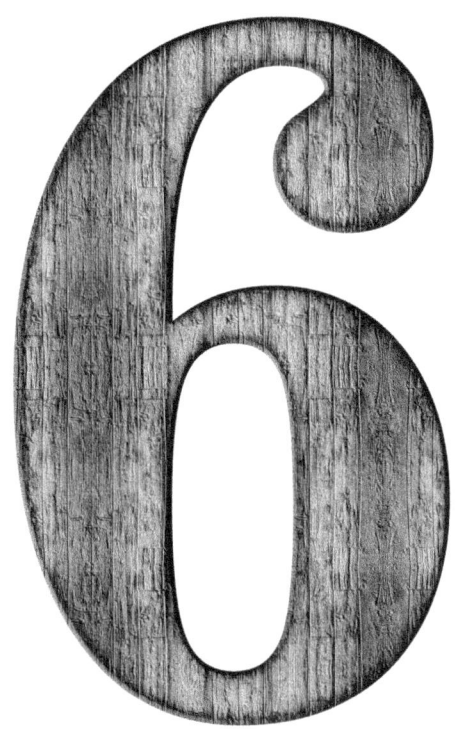

Attributes

Positive – Conscientious, Reliever, Generous, Stable, Dedicated, Idealist, Intelligent, Convenient, Worried about Home.

Negative – Suffocated, Palpation, Worried, Inexorable, Intolerant, Carefree, Unreliable, Martyrized, Discontent.

Correspondents

LETTERS: F, O, X

NUMBERS: 15, 24, 33, 42, 51, 60, 69, 78, 87, 96, 105 COLOR: Blue

GEMSTONES: Sapphire Blue, Pearl White-Blue, Diamond

CRYSTALS: Indicolite (Blue Tourmaline)

VEGETATION: Chrysanthemum, Dandelion, Bay, Tulip, Palm, Poplar, Rosewood.

FOOD: Potatoes, Spaghetti, Sweet potato, Pork, Fish, Siri, Rye bread, Parsley, Orange, Banana, Peach.

INSTRUMENTS/MUSICAL APPEAL: Banjo, Harmonica, Concert, Hymn, Musical.

PLANET: Jupiter

MONTH: June

DAYS OF BIRTH: 6, 15, 24

DAYS OF THE WEEK: Sunday, Monday, Friday

GENERAL COMPATIBILITY NUMBERS: 2, 3, 4, 9 (8 IN LOVE)

INCOMPATIBILITY NUMBERS: 1, 5, 7, 8

Note: When the individual is challenged with the number 6, these descriptions go from positive to negative until the challenge is balanced. Please be sure to read the meaning of the challenge number.

Challenges Of The Number 6

This is the challenge of accountability, obligations to personal relationships, and emotional decisions. It is rooted in too little or insufficient family and community focus in childhood. Parents, siblings, and generations of ancestors may have overweighed the child's morals, ethics, and standards. There may have been no household responsibility and unity at an early age. The child may have been encouraged to be too mature or, then, to have been heavily protected.

Challenge 6 people may feel selfish when he or she does not feel like taking on loads that are overweight. The adult with this challenge volunteers too much, gives many hunches and grieves with everything. If the bearer of challenge 6 sacrifices himself too much, he becomes selfish and controversial and feels himself a martyr. In these circumstances, he loses his talent for fostering loving, peaceful, and fruitful relationships.

As adults, they seek the needy and are sought after by them. They emit vibrations that stimulate dependency and rebel when they find themselves in bondage. It's the office or leisure club volunteers who teach and help without being asked. But when they take responsibility for a whole project and do more than they can, they feel used. The result is that nobody appreciates it. Overloaded, they inadvertently lead the "users" to feel guilty.

Challenge number 6 can swing from one to the other of the following extremes until the wearer recognizes their behavior and begins new habits that stabilize their opinions.

- Very presumptuous or very insecure.
- Very firm or very weak.
- Very cynical or very loving.

- Very critical or very unconcerned.
- Very anxious or very calm.
- Very concentrated in the family or very lonely.
- Very stubborn or very complacent.
- Very intractable or too tight.
- Very harmonious or very disharmonious.
- Very protective or very suspicious.
- Very concerned or very selfish.
- Very overbearing or very dependent.
- Too worried or too irresponsible. Very paternal or very immature.

Physical Challenges of the Number 6

The list of diseases and negative habits below relates to the challenge of number 6.

- Breast Cyst
- Kidney Problems
- Colitis
- Cramp problems
- Menstrual Problems
- Dental Problems
- Fatigue
- Excess Weight
- Urinating in Pants
- Problems in the Prostate

- Hemophilia
- Stomach Problems
- Ulcer
- Hypertension

Balancing the Challenges of the Number 6

The first step in balancing the challenge is to feel free to say, "I need harmony." Allow close people to take care of their own work, have their own opinions, and take on their own duties. You are not responsible for the family, neighborhood, office employees, community, or the world.

Assume obligations when requested. When you see the need to volunteer, ask the person who needs assistance if she wants your contribution—sometimes, a temporary loan or a minute of your time is enough. Most of the needy open up, but if you feel you are inhibited, ask how you can help them.

Automotive

Youth:

As children, these people experience the impulse of number 6 to feel part of a whole, loving and caring. When rebuked, they try to calm the authorities or act as if they are hurt. These children need comforting relationships emotionally and physically to maintain a peaceful feeling. Young people, number 6, is not likely to start discussions. No, in fact, they do not interfere, they do not complain, and they are affectionate ushers. When surrounded by distant or negligent authorities on the domestic plane, they will be protective and anxious. They want and need compassionate, pertinent, and instructive leadership.

Young ethicists like to promote happiness and friendship and want to heal all mistakes. On the specific plain, poor, and personalistic idealists and artistic people can engage them almost effortlessly. It is best that parents teach them not to exaggerate their friendliness, for otherwise, after school, they may find the kitchen full of starving schoolchildren, tasting the dinner dessert. Still, disabled colleagues who appeal to the number 6 solidarity can benefit from their impulse to teach.

Maturity:

Adults number 6 want to be determined, trustworthy, and discerning. They need to find exits for good taste and use their understanding, encouraging and comforting others. In general, they want to feel loved, loved, and respected. If this goal seems a bit conventional, it is, as are the 6. However, the number 6 adults should be able to create stability from irresponsibility. After assessing problems, they are able to direct people's lives. They have sincere impulses to counsel, to do justice, and to follow the errands to the end make them superb therapists, teachers, and nurses.

One problem with self-motivation number 6 is to understand why others need solitude. They think life would be intolerable without social intercourse and a safe place to nest. Because of their close ties to the family, if they even want to be alone once in a while, they cause surprise. In this way, commercial ambitions may exist second to family obligations.

The number 6 is concerned with paying the bills, decorating the house, and making the right impression on loved ones. Your biggest goal is staying in one place and creating the reputation of being trustworthy and interacting with safe, romantic, and considerate people. The six want to love and love with gusto.

Self-Image

Youth:

When lying in bed, listening to music and thinking, "How will I grow up? How will I walk, dress, and talk?" Young people number 6 become homegrown people. They dream of leading a comfortable, hospitable, and responsible life. Boys find themselves in respectable positions in which they provide competent services, comfort others, and provide sustenance for a loving and beloved family. Girls see themselves as friends and companions who are supportive and always present when necessary and are dedicated to marriage or a position of responsibility. Children with self-image number 6 may see affectionate paternal or maternal types who cultivate family ties, manifest artistic interests, and contribute to the well-being of the community.

Young people with dreams based on the meaning of number 6 can be self-styled, and by prolonging their emotional solidarity to such an extent, they are often devastated by the attraction they feel for dependent persons. They will do everything they can to correct situations that cause problems for people who love or want to help. They seem able to create harmony in their own lives and in the lives of members of their families and community.

Maturity:

When they leave the elevator or enter a room—before the personality or intellect takes action—the number 6 adults emit vigorous, quiet and comforting vibrations. Their attitude indicates a solitary personality and legitimate solicitude. The first impression of the six is firm, sometimes artistic and always warm. If the numbers of self-motivation and self-expression are mental or introverted, the numbers 6 will look quiet and peaceful. Dress styles, posture, and attitude do not reveal their emotional or protective self-image. The number 6 adults are mature. When you live according to your self-image, the first impression you make lets you see the fall to take on the problems of others.

Self-Expression

Youth:

Not to be noisy, supportive number 6 may consciously and obsequiously become very concerned about the problems or affairs of others—the result is that any serious consideration of consideration can lead to complications or confusion. For parents who do not reveal themselves and have entrepreneurial characteristics, the 6 may seem very troublesome, nosy, and embarrassing. On the other hand, for affectionate adults and participants, they are accepted as welcome co-workers of the family. Parents can probably calm these children by giving them more domestic responsibilities.

As teens, these community-minded perfecters often receive positions of responsibility and trust. They are successful diplomats and will try to reorganize or make adjustments whenever they feel that people or things do not meet their personal standards. The 6 rarely shy away from the engagements and have passionate opinions and dramatic pronouncements that will be heard. When frustrated or hurt by disloyalty, intolerance, or pessimism, they may overeat, lose themselves by working for others or smother pets with affection. They are faithful when they are admired, but when hardened, they may be disgruntled envious and case-makers.

Destiny

Number 6s are a mix of passion and creativity. They are also caring and thoughtful. That is why professions and occupations which deal with providing care are high on their radar. Also, 6s are practical and goal-oriented. So, occupations that tend to have clearly defined goals and objectives are also especially appealing. 6s do well as a sociologist, interior decorator, vocational counselor, academic adviser, practical or licensed nurse practitioner, veterinarian, hospital administrator, student, teacher, assistant professor, social worker, costume designer, etc.

Maturity:

The 6 have the potential to be rewarded financially for their ability to provide services, to assume responsibilities, and to be trusted employees and just employers. Still, they can be recognized for their talent of providing comfort, integrity, and dominance of the scene when needed or requested. In particular, they attract positions that require rapport, trustworthiness, and compliance.

Personal Year

The number 6 is the sixth cycle of nine years of experience that results in the accuracy and qualification of performance based on the goals outlined in the first year. It's time to focus on the responsibilities of the home, family, and community. One should keep in mind the freedom of the previous year when April initiates new projects and consciously accommodate loved ones and acquaintances on the occasion of requests. And a receptive period filled with domestic tasks and maintenance obligations. It is better to welcome what appears. "What goes around," and this year, you cannot expect to suffice yourself or receive love without repaying it. This year will have as a center the comfort of others, and personal adjustments should be made to the chronological changes produced in the previous October. And a year in which progress is measured by emotional generosity, and in November the bread thrown into the waters will return.

The personal year number 6 is called the wedding year. Whether you are marrying a person or a job, your commitments must now be given top priority. One must plan the future, live each day as if it were the last and not go to bed angry. One must make the decision to clear the differences at the end of each day and to greet the morning, free of hostility. The stripped-down attitude is very significant. Although it is better to expect to be asked, assistance can be provided when necessary. Social activities or trips should be centered on family and community projects, as there are no new directions indicated. It is time to deepen the bonds and preserve the predicates.

Personal Month

Personal month number 6 in any one-year period gives the individual the opportunity to focus on loved ones and the responsibilities of home and community.

Traveling is not advisable unless you are visiting family. Emotional receptivity, improvements, and preservation of peaceful relationships should be given top priority. Intellectual, intolerant, and self-aware views must be put aside. The previous month has given you the chance to get out of the rut, and now it's time to fix yourself, to deepen love and create harmony.

Personal Day

Wake up early and address the hourly responsibilities with a demonstration of integrity. Perform each task with determination and awareness. Do not try. Dress for the purpose of doing things and feeling comfortable. Be prepared to be held accountable for all the facts and observations, but also remember that this day is to show love and affection by taking on the problems of the weak or needy. Expect to make personal adjustments when needed, without turning work into a burden. Show the world the lover, partner or realistic, caring, and supportive friend that you are.

Make a personal commitment to go where you need help. Embrace someone and disconcert people with sincere concern and practical advice. Set aside time for domestic shopping and to visit family or some sick friend. Today is the day to focus on rejoicing others. Delays in tomorrow's communications and reduction of physical energy give you the opportunity to analyze past or future goals and to use personal time for self-evaluation.

Chapter 11: Number 7 – Mental Analysis

Attributes

Positive – Analytical, Authoritarian, Mystical, Meticulous, Introspective, Aristocratic, Logical, Haughty, Researcher, Wise.

Negative – Offensive, Caustic, Cynical, Coarse, Uncouth, Critical, Superficial.

Correspondents

LETTERS: G, P

NUMBERS: 16, 25, 34, 43, 52, 61, 70, 79, 88, 97, 106

COLOR: Purple (Violet)

GEM: Alexandrite (Amethyst)

CRYSTALS: Amethyst, Rutile violet:

VEGETATION: Saffron, Geranium, Marigold, Poppy, Fern

FOODS: Herring, Omelette, Spinach, Roasted Pork, Goose, Blackberry.

INSTRUMENTS/MUSICAL APPEAL: Harp, Ballet

PLANET: Mercury

MONTH: July

DAYS OF BIRTH: 7, 16, 25

DAYS OF THE WEEK: Saturday, Sunday

GENERAL COMPATIBILITY NUMBERS: 7 (Friendship), 5 (Business)

INCOMPATIBILITY NUMBERS: 1, 3, 6, 8, 9

Note: When the individual is challenged with the number 7, these descriptions will go from positive to negative until the challenge is balanced. Please be sure to read the meaning of the challenge number.

Challenges of the Number 7

This is the challenge to the individual's ability to accept worldly realities and keep faith in himself. It is rooted in a children's environment that did not recognize the intellectual curiosity of the child or that could not finance formal education for them.

Parents may have felt socially insecure, or the young man may have intuitively realized that his family or his right to live was surrounded by certain mysteries that should have to do with that little lettering of legal documents. The facts of health, sensibility, or commercials were illusory or nebulous, and emotional responses were rationed. The information ambushed beneath the surface, and for the young man, everything resulted in loneliness, disillusionment, and disgust.

Parents and authorities may have based their values on superficial or commercial achievements, while the child's value system was structured on the grounds of inquiry, quality, and wisdom. The child with challenge number 7 responds to stress by introverting himself into a solitary secret that coherently or reads between the lines or takes everything literally.

In youth, the individual is likely to hamper their relationships because of a reserved, emotionally blank, and critical attitude. As an adult, challenge # 7 must learn to accept the earth-down, aggressiveness, and openness of others. You must learn to live in a world where everyone belches, sometimes they eat with the wrong fork, and the average person does not have the patience to seek the hidden truths. As children, individuals with challenge number 7, abandoned to their goals, become book moths or tend to join a select intellectual group. They see themselves alone against the vulgar herd, and they feel rebellious, secretive, and arrogant when exposed to rude, coarse, or opaque people who do not understand them in a different orbit.

The number 7 challenge bearer holds a secret intruder-proof self and feeds the fear of merging or losing himself in passionate alliances, even if someone has already penetrated his skin and touched his heart. He can marry but, when he tells his secret to the other, he usually does it to the wrong person. He can stifle communication when he acts in a very detached or authoritarian way. They can take refuge in meditation or subtly hide your emotions in material interests. In other words, 7 is able to enter into a state of mind that guarantees your privacy. Until these individuals recognize the desire to improve their circumstances, they may not be absorbed by the quality of life. The 7s balance their challenge when communicating thoughts to acquaintances, develop a sense of material self-worth and have enough faith to follow their own intuition. Business evolution will have frustrating beginnings and disruptions until the 7th becomes a specialist or an authority.

Those with this challenge have a unique talent for mental games that suggest extracorporeal experience. Still, in pursuit of perfection, these individuals observe their own acts and behaviors and often think they are the only ones who can criticize.

Lowering guard, forming isolating mannerisms, and abandoning erroneous and self-deprecating ideas is more difficult for the bearer of this challenge than it is for anyone else. The bearer of this challenge habitually fears the impropriety of solitude and poverty, and his escape resources often leave him helpless, make him his own scarecrow. These and other introspective habits prevent you from engaging in activities outside your own envelope. He is asked to replace imaginary fears and skepticism by faith in himself and in humanity. The challenge of number 7 implies that the disadvantages of the individual are self-imposed and unjustified, when in fact the 7 is well-endowed intellectually and spiritually.

Challenge number 7 can swing from one to the other of the following extremes until new habits are established that stabilize the repression experienced by its bearer.

- Very critical or very incompetent.
- Very investigative or very opaque.
- Very squeaky or too off.
- Very naive or very skeptical.
- Very authoritarian or very credulous.
- Very secretive or very open.
- Very uncertain or very safe.
- Very bookish or very uncultured.
- Very perceptive or very mystified.
- Very aristocratic or very rude.
- Very patient or very rushed.
- Too deep or too careless.
- Too distant or too greedy.
- Very complex or very simple.
- Too rational or too silly. Too fast or too slow.

Physical Challenges of the Number 7

Challenges can affect physical as well as mental health. Body chemistry changes when individuals are stressed, and when we do not know what is good for us, our minds detonate anxious, angry, or frustrated habits. When we mistreat ourselves, we become sick. The individual's attitude sends a message to the brain, which tells the body to scream for help.

In order to draw attention to their malaise, people often get sick or form negative habits. Numerologists believe that illness and well-being depend on attitude, and challenges indicate attitudes that result from needy feelings. When we do not feel needy, we feel good and balanced and do not beg for the attention of others. Essentially, if the personality challenges are balanced, also the body chemistry is balanced and therefore, the risk of mental or physical illness is small.

Challenge numbers indicate the ways in which people punish themselves unconsciously for not being consciously good about themselves.

This list of illnesses and negative habits relates to the challenge of number 7.

- Addiction
- Lumbar Problems
- Adenoid Problems
- Alcoholic Personality
- Allergies
- Anemia
- Arteriosclerosis
- Blood Pressure
- Cysts in Breasts
- Cold
- Cramp
- Unruly Depression
- Diagnostic Difficulty

- Menstrual Problems
- Nausea
- Neck Problems
- Problems in Prostate

Balancing the Challenges of the Number 7

The first step in balancing the challenge is to feel free to say, "I must have faith." Discover an area of concentration in which to deepen and gain experience. Academic credits count, but they are not the only path of specialization.

The best way to build faith in yourself and others is to wake up each morning to a job you love. If you are willing to follow learning or research, and if there are time and integrity invested in your goal, you will be qualified. His talent for accuracy, originality, and research attracts other professionals with good taste and insight. If you make a commitment, you'll find friends among your peers.

To balance this challenge, it is necessary to follow what is called your intuition, first thought, or foreboding. An important part of his special ability is to use his inner resources. Do not be intimidated by titles, politics, or self-promotion. Listen to the advice of well-selected professionals and then do what you feel is best. Remember that you do not have to answer to anyone but yourself; therefore, if there is a conflict between your foreboding and logic, follow your foreboding. You will discover that you are your best friend and guide.

Sadness, melancholy, and flight from reality are habits that can be stopped. When the bearers of this challenge meet goals, people always come to share their thoughts, and mistrust, repression, and denunciations disappear, taking away the stress induced by negativism. Challenge 7 bearers can build faith in humanity when they share their inner insights and capacities. The answer encourages self-confidence, and the resulting changes in personality can be miraculous. Nothing works better here than the combination of sixth sense and common sense. When they fail to expect perfection of themselves and of humanity, the doors open to self-esteem and self-help. The challenge will be mitigated when these individuals realize that perfection can only be found on another cosmic plane. And in that, nobody is perfect!

Automotive

Youth:

For children number 7, the greatest impulse is to be observant, quiet, and questioning. When rebuked, these children become recluses, hide and cry alone. Young people number 7 are trustworthy, intuitive and solitary. When surrounded by superficial, gregarious, and overly emotional authorities, they shut them up. They want calm, refined and rational leadership, and they need toys that stimulate the intellect to satisfy their curious minds.

Parents can describe their number 7 children as deliberate, rational, and studious. These words describe these individuals when they are surrounded by learned, observant, and mature authorities. If the introspective personality of Number 7 is considered odd, and parents disregard their need to meditate, these children may become reticent and reluctant to reveal their thoughts. Young people number 7 want to investigate, read books, and discuss their observations on a technical level—this is when they come to reveal their perceptions. If these children, who have difficulty expressing their feelings, receive demonstrations of affection and love, they become more animated and authoritarian. Generally speaking, these young people are secretive, particularly as regards their sensitivity and their emotional reactions.

Children number 7 need permission to create their own world: their innate wisdom must be taken seriously and channeled into mental activities. Going to the library, harp lessons and opportunities to listen to classical music will be stimuli to your already avid intellects. The 7 acquire knowledge by investigating the topics that interest them. They will not have a large group of friends, nor will they socialize spontaneously, and very few relationships with their peers in their youth can be a problem. Children number 7 are discriminating and prefer solitude to boring companies. By turning to spiritual or intellectual pursuits, quiet, inspiring, or theoretical conversations with older, read people should satisfy any desire they may have for social intercourse. Willing number 7 likes silence, peace, and solitude. These individuals may be at the forefront of the class academically but may be socially immature. The 7 may be shy, self-absorbed, and defensive when with classmates, preferring to ignore retrograde educational procedures, abstain from parties, and invent their own mind games. On the whole, intimacy causes them discomfort.

The 7 are aristocratic loners who become melancholy when surrounded by rudeness and people who push them to materialistic priorities. Surprisingly, they fear loneliness, but they make it difficult to get to know others. When they are sure of the facts surrounding them, and only there, the 7 enter into the conversation. Parents should expose them to the intricacies of photography, computers, and the world of metaphysics to direct their interest and keep them occupied.

Young people, number 7 need to wear cotton shirts, sweaters that do not scream and be in contact only with the best that exists. Of 10 dresses in the hanger of a store, girl number 7, without the intention of cunning, chooses the most expensive and the best made. When they buy school notebooks, boys automatically choose the most effective and best made. These children feel comfortable with the quality and prefer to satisfy a desire rather than a bunch of commitments.

It is best to teach young people number 7 early on to accept human frailty and their own imperfections. The chatterboxes, the manual labor, and the sports they demand from the physicist do not appeal to them, and they tend to be brainstorming researchers who perceive the world with reservations and think harder before accepting a job. Classical technical, scientific, or academic education will be of great help to these children, and any specialization will be the target for them to feel at ease. The numbers 7 fit into many professional, refined, and reserved groups of people.

The 7 are perfectionists who reach maturity by carefully dissecting every detail of their lives before proceeding. If the 7 have more conventional numerical meanings in other aspects of their maps, they may not be introverts. However, they are likely to find a way to preserve respect for their privacy.

As teenagers, deftly, the 7 do one thing at a time. When adults who seek the truth, they want all the information available before making any decisions. Alert parents understand that these sedentary analysts are indeed listening to the music of the spheres. The number 7 rarely has a sense of urgency or obsession with material goods. They attract money, recognition, and influential alliances as they follow their natural instincts to question everything.

Maturity:

Number 7 adults want to be purists undisturbed by practical realities or worldly people. They need to be surrounded by timeless treasures and may seem disconnected from the world most of the time. They want to be perceptive, contemplative, and scholarly. Your desires and accomplishments form a category by itself.

People number 7 do not like to surround themselves with busy businesspeople, noisy phones, or cliché typewriters. Lovers seldom gregarious or excited, knowing that they do not need to express constant demonstrations of affection, produce the perfect criteria for the patient soul mate. The 7 do not feel comfortable when they are expected to be obsessed with sensuality or when they are pressured into a demanding social whirlwind. On the other hand, any theoretical discussion, any enlightening television program, or sophisticated recipe leaves us intrigued.

When unbalanced, these individuals may want a desperate escape. They may be obsessive fanatics or aggressive dreamers on the commercial plane. When balanced, they are rational, discerning, and conscientious originals. When under the care of number 7, young people learn to be inquiring, meticulous, and resourceful. Capable of following their natural instincts, the number 7 adults are astute, broad-minded, and haughty parents.

One thing you can expect from a balanced, resourceful, thoughtful, and patient figure is figuring out how to attract things or lovers that fit your expectations. It is very improbable to find balanced self-motivation 7 that is self-satisfied, openly affectionate, and can be instigated by dramatic means.

Those who have self-motivation number 7 have problems with feelings of introspection, melancholy, and emotional poverty.

They tend to fear their own desire for separatism. The 7 do not like to live quiet, but they cannot be true to themselves in routinely competitive business environments. When you follow the natural instincts to become academics, professionals, and experts, the prospects of financial success are good. In spiritual or metaphysical pursuits, the 7 are attuned to the mastery of the deeper truths, and their discoveries can be extraordinary.

Self-Image

Youth:

When lying in bed, listening to music and thinking, "How will I grow up? How will I walk, dress, and talk?" Young people number 7 become aristocrats. They dream of leading a serene life of quality, free to investigate, select, and analyze. The boys see themselves as authoritarian, lecturing on the favorite specialty for their intellectual peers, and the girls see themselves as the reincarnation of Margaret Mead or Madame Curie, surrounded by silent and serious students in a room of shelves full of bound books or in a laboratory wide and perfect. Children with self-image number 7 may see themselves as proud, dignified, and confident royalty—above the mundane and low-hanging obligations of youth—and are usually called princes or princesses.

The 7 may appear to be self-assured, thoughtful, and quiet children who have the intellectual ability to meddle with their elders. When the number 7 says they want to be scientists, photographers, or priests, they find themselves in the right position to use their erudite, technical, or mystical ideas. When they live according to self-image, these individuals will be the first to read the recipe of a dish, following every ingredient and instruction, and criticize the dish after savoring the fruit of the work they attribute to others. These children, these teens or young adults, do not like to get their hands dirty or sweat at work. They seek to avoid mundane work and tend to assume the position of specialists or authorities. Young people with dreams based on the meaning of number 7 may have discriminating tastes. They are difficult to please, and they enforce physical, mental, and spiritual privacy. Its overall appearance is coordinated carefully, with pastels and light materials. They are not inclined to call attention, so they use classic styles instead of wanting to affirm fashion. When in tune with self-image, they have a sense of style so harmonious that it impresses, and they dress and dress impeccably.

The 7 rarely seem emotionally expressive or mercenary. The youthful expectations of number 7 are not sensual or materially ambitious. Not; for this haughty self-image, intimate desire is centered on solitary inquiry, analysis, and deductions based on the world above, below, and around you.

Maturity:

When leaving the elevator or entering a room—before the personality or intellect comes into action—the adult with the self-image 7 emits dignified and refined vibration. His attitude indicates a reserved personality and haughtiness. The first impression she makes is serene, sometimes curious, and always of good lineage. When self-expression and self-expression numbers are outgoing or unconventional, the number 7 uses unique color combinations and looks decidedly fancy.

The number 7 adults perceive themselves to be experts or critics and can be very quick to guess. When they live according to self-image, the first impression can intimidate, and may not relate well to all.

The number of self-expression can govern the first impression as long as utilitarian or flashy costumes are indicated by the vocational descriptions delineated in the meaning of the number. The number of self-motivation can influence the wearer's wear as long as they are relaxed and doing what they want to do. However, when these individuals live by self-image, they will not display corresponding colors or styles indicated by the numbers elsewhere on their numerological map.

Self-Expression

Youth:

Adults find it obvious when children have self-expression number 7 since in youth, the talents 7 are based on questioning everything: in asking why the sky is blue and why birds fly. Because they do not accept superficial explanations and investigate all the answers, the 7 keep the parents mentally alert and send the teachers to the reference library. When they grow up, they research hobbies, read for hours, and enjoy playing or listening to stringed instruments. They leave the authorities perplexed and push away the less introspective equals. Helpful, Accurate, perceptive, and in search of truth, these children add refinement to the family project. It's hard not to be surprised by their intelligence and meticulousness.

Not wanting to be rude, a logical number 7 can take a thorough and penetrating attitude to rules and regulations. Every original and well-founded criticism must be discussed in a persistent and ingenious way. Flexible, insatiable, and industrious fathers may seem too demanding, pretentious, or shrewd. For educated, calm, and cerebral adults, the instinctive nobility of purpose, intellectual curiosity, and the sincerity of 7 are expected and welcomed. The need to investigate the children, to get to the root of everything, will be respected.

As a teenager, these bookish perfectionists can close themselves in concentration and set impervious to noise, hunger, or fun. Despite their general disregard for light jokes and conventional social interactions, they are capable of eloquent speech or hilarious humor when they are on their whim. New puns, mathematical logic games, cameras, and computers can fascinate them. They are intellectuals and should take every opportunity to use their sharp brains. Museums, ancient ruins, and everything that justify a photograph will give them the opportunity to develop artistic interests. They are not sloppy, disinterested, or amateurish, and seek the scientific or technical approach when researching on their own.

Observers, number 7 discriminators hesitate and do not speak or assume leadership roles without being sure of the facts. They may prefer to be used as accessories, but as soon as they find a professional interest that offers mental challenges, refined environment and opportunity to work independently, the 7 demonstrate to be knowledgeable quality experts.

In their youth, the 7 prefer light fabrics, tasteful clothes, and fine, well-prepared foods. Once they discover the things that work in their favor, they do not make changes. In general, the 7 disregards the novelties, the nonsense, and the dramatic displays of emotion. Feel at ease with non-competitive subjects where you do not need to follow the crowd or dress uniformly. The 7 do not feel comfortable when they are highlighted, prefer a lower profile, and ignore the less evolved opinions. They seem to do everything in a hurry, and during crises, they try to control their emotions and act cool.

Children, adolescents, and young people should deserve privacy and be encouraged to see all sides of everything. They can learn, with books and recognized authorities, to become scientists, technicians, or leading spiritual leaders.

Maturity:

Self-expression number 7 has the potential to reward itself financially because of the ability to investigate all aspects of a subject, to perfect techniques, and to discover the findings with confidence. It is possible to recognize the superior intuition and talent of number 7 to appreciate or produce quality work. The 7 draw positions that require specialized information and in which sharp perception is convenient. Your communications are deliberate, precise, and logical. These researchers are sincere, patient, and undisturbed. The 7 become the center of attention when they probe an idea and prove its worth.

Innate mystical talents often make researchers look eccentric. They should seek wisdom without forgetting worldly needs, financial stability, and domestic responsibilities. Mental capture explorations and fascination with spirit sessions and para-sciences often prevent the innate parapsychic from concentrating on the accumulation of practical assets.

In general, the 7 will not be escapists. However, the negative aspects of this number indicate teasing, melancholy, and dismay when finances go badly, and relationships tax their emotions. Unfortunately, these introspective talents are not likely to discuss their emotional issues. They may seem sloppy or disconnected, but they actually feel everything in depth. The 7 find it difficult to trust others, so they seek information within themselves. When balanced, whoever has self-expression number 7 knows when to act based on careful consideration.

Destiny

The insightful and perceptive nature of 7s enables them to work well in professions that require deep insight and understanding in to the feelings of others and the structures of the world. Also, 7s will gravitate toward creative professions in which great courage is needed to innovate. Suggested Occupations: Psychiatrist, psychologist, psychotherapist, scientist, specialist technician, engineer, computer programmer, systems analyst, mathematician, editor, judge, photographer, underwater explorer, oceanographer, geologist, historian, etc.

Personal Year

The number 7 is the seventh of the nine-year cycle of experiences that results in the agility and performance qualification based on the goals set in the first year. It is time to rest, reflect, and analyze. Let go of the domestic and emotional sacrifice of the previous year. March usher in an age of personal values, non-commercial approaches, and self-analysis as the spring and summer months do not lead to commercial ambitions or physical overload.

For most, it's a slow year, filled with delays in communication, legal issues, and unexpected feelings of loneliness. For the others, the year focuses on a path of specialized studies that was decided to take place in October of the previous year. And introspective year, convenient to the examination of the past and the planning of the future. Money and practical achievements will appear as long as the individual is not very mutant or aggressive.

Do not be afraid to pass business or material interests to the background. Recognize this experience, unique in nine years, to see life, choose priorities, and learn from the past. Do not move. Keep calm. Do not rush the stations or handle the days. The most promising plans will work under control, or you let in things that might be beneficial. If aggressive attitudes are taken, the financial and material activities to come will be delayed. Problems arise that force you to think about why you have been feeling helpless or repressed. A serene attitude is beneficial. It is not important whether you understand the way things will happen for the better: it is important to hope for the best, to have faith and to take rest from external responsibilities and ambitions. This year aims to remind you that life is not just what you see.

Personal year number 7 encourages the development of new interests and deeper understandings. The ideas generate investigations that materialize in the commercial achievements of the following year. In order to gain mobility and freedom to pursue commercial or material ambitions the following year, health is a factor to be considered now. Medical and dental reviews should be planned before July as preventive measures. Any physical malaise must be identified and immediately referred to a professional. If the intellectual, spiritual or physical preparations are ignored, it is because the year is not being used wisely. Intuitive decisions that have been made and archived for future use will determine the scope of maturity harvested in the last six months.

Personal Month

Personal month number 7 in any one year provides the opportunity to question the plans, enlist the help of professionals and learn from the past. Attitudes should be taken only the following month. Wait, and you will see that the answers you will have are appropriate for legal negotiations, questionable alliances, and current progressive ideas. A broad, inquisitive and demanding point of view must have absolute priority. Aggressiveness, commercial ambitions, and unnecessary social interactions must be put aside. Remember to say, "I'll think." Examine others' opinions carefully and think before you speak. Do not reveal your thoughts; be a little secretive. This is not a good time to get a phone call. When the phone rings, you will receive data. Take time to read, self-test and savor philosophical discussions. Be patient, tolerant, and feel like spending time in silence. This can be an exceptionally illuminated month.

Personal Day

Wake up with a leisure attitude, do not overload the physical, and avoid confusion or conflict. Address each experience with calm, serenity, and posture. Whatever the task, focus on preparation and accuracy. Review to get the most out of a situation. Be receptive and listen to the ideas of others. It is a day of lingering long in personal plans, character traits, and the non-material side of expectations. Commercial delays or technical issues will overwhelm, solutions will not be readily available, and arrangements for solving problems must be made only tomorrow.

Today, other people are likely to postpone making commitments or living up to their promises. An expected phone call or letter may not arrive. But the moon will continue to rise, and the sun will set as usual, despite the stumbling of the day. It is best to remain passive and not be disturbed by what happens. If possible, continue reading informative books, go to the movies or let the imagination roam freely when listening to music. The practical problems will solve themselves.

Make a personal commitment to improving yourself. Be honest and reflect on past behavior to see how to change or eliminate unproductive habits. Take some time to look happier and healthier. Your abstract thoughts can become practical accomplishments if you are inspired and have faith. Take care of medical or dental obligations. Talk to a psychologist, lawyer, or accountant if you need professional knowledge. Gain knowledge and give advice to others—without thinking of compensation. Tomorrow's concentration on efficiency, life force, and material goals will bring the opportunity for tangible results.

Chapter 12: Number 8 – Material Power

Attributes

Positive – Efficient, Reliable, Strong, Self-Ambitious, Discerning, Insightful, Functional, Affirmative, Intelligent.

Negative – Materialist, Intolerant, Tired, Dishonest, Disheartened, Undisciplined, Thirsty for Power, Sullen, Coarse

Correspondents

LETTERS: H, K, Z

NUMBERS: 26, 35, 44, 53, 62, 71, 80, 89, 98, 107

COLOR: Pink, Reddish-Pink, Mauve

GEM: Diamond

CRYSTAL: Pyrite, Morganite Pink Beryl Rosy

VEGETATION: Begonia, Dahlia, Jasmine, Nogueira Pine Tree, Rhododendron

FOODS: Cereals, Bacon, Rice, Cauliflower, Chicken, Tea, Apple Pie

INSTRUMENTS/MUSICAL APPEAL: Hawaiian Guitar, Coral, Soprano, Theatre of Magazine

MUSICAL NOTE: Acute

PLANET: Sun

MONTH: August

DATEDAYS OF BIRTH: 8, 17, 26

DAY OF THE WEEK: Thursday

GENERAL COMPATIBILITY NUMBERS: 2, 4, 6

INCOMPATIBILITY NUMBERS: 7, 8, 9

Note: When the individual bears the challenge of number 8, these descriptions are no longer positive to negative until the challenge is balanced. Please be sure to read the meaning of the number of the code.

Challenges of the Number 8

This is the challenge to the individual's understanding of the values and purposes of money and power. As children, the bearers of this challenge may have seen authorities with unreasonable ambitions that focused on the financial picture. Power at a high level and competitive spirit were the only means available to achieve freedom—or the opposite extreme may have been tried, and in this case, the authorities may have had no interest in accumulating assets, in influencing the competitiveness. Either of these extremes gave young people 8 false sense of material values and fostered a greater or lesser obsession with material possessions and financial security. As a consequence, the individual bearers of the challenge usually become self-employed or self-destructive, without a goal.

As adolescents, individuals with this challenge may excel in sports, school work, or part-time employment after school hours. They may be considered super-young or, at the opposite extreme, these adolescents may become unreasonable, incoherent, and unrelated. They may be unable to make good judgments, to order their affairs, or to take responsibility for managing time, money, and practical obligations. For those with this challenge, the concern with self-control is either too much, or insufficient. Or they are gales, or breezes, with temperaments compatible with each end.

These individuals may think, "Who will reject me if I have money, power, and prestige?" However, responses tell them that people cannot be treated as if they are business structures. Certain 8 should learn that there is a power superior to the board. To master the challenge of 8, one must first master the challenge of number 7, who has faith in non-material values and recognizes the wisdom in every man.

Challenge number 8 can move from one to the other of the following extremes until it is recognized and begin new habits that stabilize the material ambitions of its bearer.

- Very combative or very apathetic.
- Very unruly or very ethical.
- Very aggressive or very slow.
- Very ambitious or very chaotic.
- Very efficient or very incompetent.
- Too defensive or too defenseless.
- Very controllable or very unreliable.
- Very limited or very expansive.
- Very sloppy or very upright.
- Too forgetful or too conscious.
- Very busy or very lazy.
- Very dynamic or very fragile.
- Very wasteful or very parsimonious. Very exhibitionist or very careless.

Physical Challenges of the Number 8

This list of diseases and negative habits is related to the challenge of number 8.

- Addictions
- Herpes
- Alcoholism
- Indigestion

- Allergy
- Clutches at the joints
- Appendicitis
- Laryngeal Asthma
- Nervousness
- Cold
- Skin Problems
- Eczema
- Disk
- Herniation Epilepsy
- Smoking Problems
- Eye Problems
- Fainting Spells
- Varicose Veins
- Heart Problems
- Warts
- Hepatitis

Balancing the Challenges of the Number 8

The first step in balancing the challenge is to feel free to say, "I need material freedom." Take a look at personal relationships. Do not forget to thank the secretary for the consideration shown outside the job specifications. Invite a friend over for a formal lunch. Set a goal to organize your time to include a hobby, a nimble walk, or a quiet night with loved ones. Force yourself to read books that speak of the lives of billionaires and ask yourself if money actually bought them all.

Keep in mind that you find the same people you encountered on the climb as descending. Be generous, considerate, and respect people for what they do. It is impossible to accomplish anything in a world full of caciques. Every cacique needs loyal Indians to take care of the details, so protect your tribe and make it happy.

Automotive

Youth:

As a child, the number 8 feels a tremendous drive to be attentive, self-reliant, and active. When rebuked, this child can avail himself of a well-kept treasure, stare confidently, and exchange tricks to relieve his wounded ego. This child needs exercises, practical tasks and interactions with peers, as the young number 8 is generally courageous, managerial, and decisive. When surrounded by weak or unreasonable authorities, crack the whip. You want discipline, and you figure out how to do it.

Children number 8 need to plan, build, and work consistently. His cleverness, ability to concentrate, and intellectual curiosity must be coordinated with physical activities. Lack of interest in artistic self-expression or the difficulty in accepting the vulnerability of others can be a problem in maturity. The 8 are born organizers and fall to convince everyone to help them. By virtue of his ability to see the intimacy of unrealistic people and his outspoken criticism, his parents, if they wish to avoid disrespectful confrontations, must practice what they teach, or find out that their children are directing them.

Maturity:

The number 8 adults want to own and enjoy all that money can buy. They strive to be influential and lead a well-organized and constructive lifestyle, preferring traditional marriage, and creating a family that shares their ambitions. However, these 8 are the self-mediators who have no respect for weakness, procrastination, or failure. They may, therefore, have no eyes for the partner's emotional anxieties or for the concepts of relaxed holidays or non-organizational social activities.

People number 8 do not like to be disobeyed, disorganized, or distracted by small details. Since they are seldom content to pay the bills, they prefer to gravitate to the big businessmen. The 8 must have the latest Gucci wallet, the latest Mercedes-Benz model, or some other prestige accessory. These individuals can swim 20 laps in a pool, lift weights or run 20 kilometers before or after work. They have formidable vitality and physical stamina, and therefore need leaks to relieve stress—which they seem to nurture. Rest or relax, on the other hand, annoys you.

Balanced 8 will take success seriously. Nervous schemes and sloppy work habits indicate fear of failure and the underlying inability to self-govern. The Balanced 8 believes that it takes money to make money, and his approach to finances is realistic and conscientious. However, this perception does not compensate for its possible blindness with respect to the intimate ones that offer him love and consolation.

Self-Image

Youth:

When lying in bed, listening to music and thinking, "How will I grow up? How will I walk, dress and talk?" the 8-year-old pre-teens envision an industrial giant, the host of the major sports, an immortal sportsman. They dream of being CEOs at some board, going out after lunch for a business talk on the company's yacht, or receiving the Sportsman of the Year trophy or training to death a winning team. Children with the self-image number 8 look rich and, above all, winners—CEOs, professional athletes, and financial advisors.

Maturity:

When they leave the elevator or enter a room—before the personality or intellect comes into action—the number 8 adults emit a marked, benign and impertinent vibration. His attitude indicates a strong personality and seems to exude energy. The first impression they make is thriving, domineering, and dignified. When the meanings of numbers of self-motivation and self-expression are artistic or modest, they display the symbols of prestige, and their dress style, posture, and attitude signal to the world that they do not cost cheap.

Self-Expression

Youth:

The number 8 talents lead the child to work early. They will be more competent, consistent, and more effective adults if they are encouraged to manage finances, time, and energy properly. To reach the ambitious goals they draw for themselves, they need affirmation, workmanship, and life force. However, once they have the opportunity to solve their practical problems on their own, the number 8 children demonstrate that they trust in themselves.

As a teenager and young adult, the 8 are always busy and must learn to relax, have good school grades, play on the varsity, become a class president, and make money after school. They have a talent for big business. These young people are serious finance students and have the knack of getting a return to their physical and commercial efforts.

Maturity:

When 8s are able to become centered in their chosen profession, they age well into it. They tend to become industry experts and innovators. They can find ways of improving processes and finding dimensions to their chosen areas which others may not have been able to find. 8s tend to have success later on in their career since all those years of cumulative study and reflection lead them to attain a degree of mastery that very few are able to achieve.

8s have the potential to be rewarded financially for their executive ability, their efficiency, and their commercial practice. It is possible to be recognized for its vital force and physical coordination. The 8 are domineering personalities who plan, organize, and work to make the most of their efforts. These individuals emit vibrations that puts them in the driver's armchair.

Number 8's must recognize their need to maintain a positive approach. In a business or sports environment, they are reservoirs of solutions to problems that radiate force. When asked to socialize and promote, the 8 have the skills to delight and impress the most prestigious clients. They are persuasive opportunists when they know what they want—and usually, know it. And it is possible to count that the balanced number 8 will be employees and conscious employers. They demonstrate impertinent style and position in their attire and enjoy displaying an air of prosperity, power, and ability.

Destiny:

The high degree of conscientiousness of 8s leads them to excel in jobs that require tenacity and resiliency. They are also geared toward occupations which require a profound study of the subject matter at hand. Here are some of the best occupations for 8s: manufacturer, banker, stockbroker, financial adviser, professional sportsman, military officer, statistician, accountant, office manager, engineer, band conductor, drummer, business lawyer, construction contractor, construction supervisor, payroll administrator, investor, cashier, controller, bank loan manager, franchise operator, collection manager, civil servant, union leader, sales manager , farmer, importer/exporter, weight lifter, physical fitness consultant, film producer, and director of theatrical production.

Personal Year

The number 8 is the eighth in the nine-year cycle of experiences that result in the predictability and performance qualification based on the goals set in the first year.

In February, the individual sows ideas that spring up in April. During the first and last weeks of September, activity intensifies, money is collected, and influential alliances. For most, finances improve, and new opportunities result from projects postponed and reviewed in the previous year.

It is the year in which you see the tangible results of past efforts. If romance is the goal, the prospects for wealth, health, and ambition are more easily realized. Single-sex flirts can uncover sparks of sexual activity in June. If marriage is the goal, it's time to hone your nerves to go out in search of a meaningful relationship. A business approach is both dating and taking control of a company. You need to ignore the petty problems and use the ability to plan and manage effectively to achieve the goals at work. It's time to go after what you want in the hope of getting it.

Personal Month

Personal month number 8, in any personal year, provides the opportunity to take control of commercial and financial affairs. You must always rely on yourself, be energetic, and resourceful. Powerful, entrepreneurial and pragmatic acquaintances are important now. It's not the time to take a holiday, sensitize or take unruly behavior. After delays, legal problems and unanswered questions from the previous month, you need to develop an efficient attitude and break the wheels of progress. The projects started seven months ago require the maximum effort: to advertise, promote and be insightful. One must dress with dignity, be diplomatic, and display all the prestige symbols available. When it is organized and persuasive, the results achieved will be exceptional.

Personal Day

Wake up to the goals in mind and propose to fulfill them. Sketch plans and expect to fulfill them. Check the expenses, be careful, and try to see far, making the day is profitable and orderly. There will be money coming in or going out on account of the bargains. Shopping, marketing ideas, and socializing for business are the favorite activities. Look successful: remember, money attracts money, and the dominant impressions attract the domain.

On-time, ask for a raise, an office with a panoramic view, or plan to travel first class. Be direct, expect to achieve results, and everything will run smoothly. Do not be ungainly, obstinate or self-indulgent. Keep your appearance dignified and affirmative and boost self-confidence. Fragile attempts, fear of failure, and offensive verbiage emit cowardly vibrations. Be brave and expect to be respected. Otherwise, the very strong energy of this day will internalize itself in the form of restrictions and frustration.

"Invest" in bookmarks if there are late payments. Today, you are more likely to receive debts or favors. Do not take risks, do not lose your temper, and do not be foolish. In strange situations, be the first to maintain refinement, confidence, and conscious leadership. Remember that whoever is in power is watching. Today's energetic, enthusiastic and forward executive efforts can bring material rewards tomorrow. Success depends on common sense, logic, and problem solving constructively. If you keep the goals in mind, it will be a memorable day.

Chapter 13: Number 9 And 0 – Conclusions

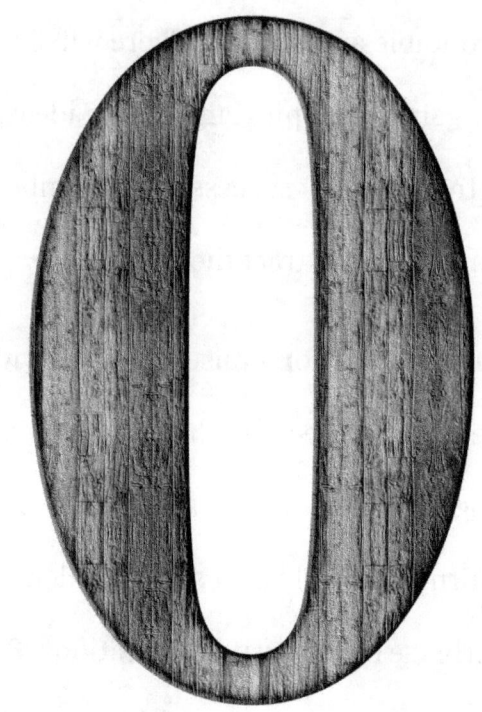

Attributes

Positive – Compassion, Empathy, Art, Faith, Generosity, Compatibility, Bravery, Tenderness, Voluntariness, Tolerance.

Negative – Bitterness, Fanaticism, Selfishness, Jealousy, Indiscrimination, Inconstancy, Coldness, Disappointment, Covetousness

Correspondents

LETTERS: I, R

NUMBERS: 18, 27, 36, 45, 54, 63, 72, 81, 90, 99, 108

COLOR: Saffron, Orange-Yellow-Gold

GEMS: Opal

CRYSTALS: Alunite

VEGETATION: Holly, Magnolia, Gold Bud, Oak, Banana

FOOD: Milk, Cheese, Beef Boi, Jelly

INSTRUMENTS/MUSICAL APPEAL: Violin, Tenor, Symphony

MUSICAL NOTE: Acute

PLANET: Aura and Influences of All or None

MONTH: September

DAYS OF BIRTH: 9, 18, 27

DAY OF THE WEEK: Monday (Only), Friday (With Friends)

NUMBERS OF GENERAL COMPATIBILITY: 5, 6, 9,1 (Artistic); 3, 8 (Business)

INCOMPATIBILITY NUMBERS: 4, 7

Note: When the individual has the challenge of number 9, these descriptions will go from positive to negative until the challenge is balanced. Please be sure to read the meaning of the challenge number.

The Challenges of the Numbers 9 and 0

This is the challenge to the individual understanding of human emotions and fragility. The bearer of this challenge is born with the maturity of an "old soul," which is philosophical and has more opportunities than the average person. So you have immediate personal choice. It has the ability to know what is wrong, how to repair it, and also great potential for compassion, empathy and solving beneficent problems.

In youth, adults may have expected too much from these young people, even more than they are able to understand or achieve. Generally speaking, these children are born to parents who have passed the average age of having children. In some cases, they are the middle children of large families, who run the tightrope because they have to obey the older, domineering brothers and father the younger brothers. A serious illness can have them hospitalized or left under the care of adults at home. These children were asked to understand serious personal problems or the emotional ups and downs of younger or older relatives who surrounded them.

When pre-teens and teens, they are loners. They can go from class to class in the pursuit of their performance models or exemplary people of an art or craft. They fall in love at a distance, have difficulty with intimate relationships, and often fall in love with passion. The 9 or 0 have so much to give that they cannot give it just to one person, or else they sink into the needs of their lovers.

Young people, number 9 can take on responsibilities, become group leaders, and nullify themselves for the welfare of their peers. As adults, they continue to give more than they receive or else face the world with selfishness. The 9, unconsciously, feel deprived of the dreamed joys of youth and try to stay young forever. They usually marry older or more educated individuals or young people, and the neediest individuals. Either they serve the community, or they live at the expense of the state; are freshmen or "old souls."

Challenge 0 can swing from one to the other of the following extremes until you are identified and begin new habits that impersonate your carrier's emotions and entice you to make choices and changes.

- Very deprived or very selfish.
- Very airy mentally or very fanatical.
- Very melodramatic or very unimpressive.
- Very satisfied or very unhappy.
- Very possessive or very liberal.
- Very dispassionate or very romantic.
- Very understanding or very hard.
- Very charitable or very greedy.
- Very brave or very cowardly.
- Very fickle or very loyal.
- Very provincial or very cultured.
- Very stubborn or very receptive.
- Very dedicated or very careless.
- Very vindictive or very forgiving.

Physical Challenges of the Numbers 9 and 0

This list of illnesses and negative habits relates to the development of Number 9 and 0.

- Problems in the Back
- Swollen Bone
- Jealousy Problems
- Bronchitis
- Problems in the Knees
- Cellulite Problems
- Lung Problems
- Problems in the Eyes
- Pneumonia
- Glandular Problems
- Sea Gout
- Problems in the Breasts
- Headaches
- Stuttering
- Cardiac arrest
- Venereal disease
- Warts

Balancing the Challenges of the Numbers 9 and 0

The first step in balancing the challenge is to feel free to say, "I need to be needed."

Select priorities, and remember that you have a good reason to follow your feelings.

Resolve your ambitions now. Be decisive, and you will receive positive responses. You have the ability to see all the options. Analyze your priorities: find an advantageous angle from which you can cultivate your compassion, solidarity, and desire to rise.

Open your heart to counter the urge to be possessive. You cannot be tied to purely domestic or community needs. You have the ability to set the example to be followed by others. But do not feel needy if your students might become your teachers. This is a great honor, and the greater credit will be yours.

Automotive

Youth:

As a child, the impulse that Number 9 feels is to be affectionate, empathetic, and jealous of your circumstances. When rebuked, this child understands the feelings of authority, becomes emotional and apologizes, or throws all the blame on the accuser. This child needs love, from sensitive social interactions, and from the sense of being needed. The young number 9 is kind, caring, and well-meaning. When surrounded by distanced authorities, he remains impassive or willful. He wants heat and goes to extremes to get it.

The 9 want to be multitalented communicators. They should explore interests in music, arts, sports, theatre, and writing. When the medium leads to spiritual or religious observation, children 9 offer an answer. However, they can transfer from one faith system to another that accumulates knowledge. The 9 tend to disseminate their interests, their beneficent efforts, and their romantic ideas. They may dream for a time that they were born to be saints. When they know that the saints have to live the hell on earth to be considered, they decide to play Helen Hayes or Richard Burton, becoming worshiped stars of the theatre.

Maturity:

The number 9 adults want to live a worthwhile life. They will find it difficult to narrow their interests and concentrate on mundane practices or immediate needs. The 9 are led to help others and to create or engage with something that has universal artistic merit. They have inspired sanitarians and altruistic reformers who want to benefit the world. They are capable of self-sacrifice even when they have little and practice great deeds for petty people. The 9 want security, but they do little to stabilize their economy, their emotions, or their movements.

People number 9 do not like being tied to the house or having their emotions suppressed. Almost always unable to confine themselves to a single intimate relationship, they have many groups of friends. The 9 should go where they are needed. A less fortunate stranger, a loss-making charity, or a theatrical company looking for actresses or audiences touches their hearts or their pockets. These individuals practice generous, sentimental, and impulsive gestures. They feel the pain of the other with a sense of immediacy difficult to be tolerated in every day for the most intimate.

Self-Image

Youth:

Lying in bed, listening to music, and thinking, "How am I going to be when I grow up? How am I going to walk, dress, and talk?" Pre-adolescent number 9 sees himself as a wise counselor, a dedicated artist, or a stripped-down humanitarian, dreams of receiving the Nobel Peace Prize and donate the money to a charity.

Self-images number 9 relate to pleasing others. They make promises and try to keep them. The first impression the 9 people make is romantic, artistic, and strong. And your youthful desire possesses the emotional and physical ability to take on everyone's problems and relieve the universal signs of suffering. At times they may seem overly dramatic. When they feel attuned to self-image, they subjugate their personalities and material ambitions to stimulate a lover or collaborate for a cause they respect.

Maturity:

When they leave the elevator or enter a room—before the personality or intellect takes action—the number 9 adults emit friendly vibrations. Often graying early, the 9 seem wise and dignified—never old and broken. His attitude indicates gracious personality and seems to exude the aura of well-intentioned interest. The first impression they make is magnetic.

When they use the saffron color—a yellow-orange mixture reminiscent of autumn leaves—the self-image is enhanced. The self-image individual number 9 need not convince or strive to persuade others to be equal to himself. In essence, 9 includes the talents of communication of the number 3, the talents of representation and communication and the communitarian services of the number 6, and the talents of teaching and communication of the theatre of the airy number 9. The first impression that causes an emotionally stimulated number 9 can be intense and passionately lively. And an expert in feeling the needs of others and playing the expected role. This impressionable idealist has the temperament of a great goddess or an eccentric artist.

The 9 are born leaders. Without experience or preparation, they join the groups and set the example that others choose to follow. When they live according to their self-image, they are affectionate, hospitable, and tolerant.

Self-Expression

Youth:

Without the intention of exaggerating, the compassionate number 9 may, in a heroic gesture, return to a burning building to save a pet or relative. The 9 think about the well-being of others, examine the general picture, and practice deprived acts. They imitate adults and copy colleagues. The 9 are funny, free-form, and fanciful. They inspire confidence and are extremely intuitive. Materialistic, possessive, narrow-minded parents may seem too emotional, generous, or expansive. For educated, artistic and broad-minded adults, the number 9 children are students and teachers who need to be enlightened at every opportunity.

Teenagers number 9 and young adults are forthright, discerning, and attractive. They have many friends and various interests that keep them away from home. These teens have distant correspondents, spend time with the old and infirm, and play Hamlet or Ophelia at the Shakespearean school festival. They are adept at words, and writing, interpreting, and talking are easy things. These children of universal love are intimidated by commercial ambitions, exclusiveness, and pessimism. They are willing to save or serve the world and need to work in a job that offers extensive benefits.

Maturity:

Individuals number 9 have the potential to financially reward themselves with the ability to communicate their understanding of human nature. They are artists of unique talent, expert interpreters who realize their abilities and establish examples worthy of note. It is possible by the recognition of their ability to empathize with people to respond to the needs of others and to delight and win great audiences. The basic attributes of number 9 are the taste for the world, the nobility of purpose, and dispossession. These individuals emit a vibration that puts them at the receiving end of the problems of others. The number 9 talents should recognize your need to inspire, teach, and overestimate others. They have a great capacity for impersonal love and charity. The business environment, the competitiveness of colleagues, and the commercial aggressiveness make us nervous and stun your creativity. The 9 are excellent in the areas of development and counseling. Sales and marketing may or may not attract them. If your profession requires diversification of attitudes, you will have the ability to make a simple sale or a solemn promotion an informal meeting. As lecturers, they are excellent, along with a wide variety of audiences. It can be said that balanced 9 are open, airy, and trustworthy. They are usually artistic, charming and neat—predicates in the organization of services or communication.

Destiny

Number 9s enjoy communicating and relating to others. They are apt to help others develop their own talents. They are also keen on improving themselves and the world. Here are some suggested occupations: Editor, writer, reporter, foreign correspondent, editor in chief, circulation manager, teacher, teacher assistant, physician, lecturer, artist, illustrator, social worker, welfare administrator, university administrator, preacher, etc.

Personal Year

The number 9 is the new year in the nine-cycle of experiences that results in the agility and performance qualification based on the goals set in the first year. In the spring, the individual receives recognition of creative efforts, takes inventory of past accomplishments, and prepares to begin new long-term goals. For the most part, old boyfriends, college mates, and personal ideals spring up and are the subject of definitive evaluation. In addition, a year to discard the clothes that went out of style, re-read the favorite books, and abandon lost loves. It is time for reflection and reassessment. This year requires unconditional love and acceptance of the problems of others. Nothing new begins, so anything that insinuates a fresh start the next year should be eliminated.

Changes are necessary, so certain things must be completed. The new targets instigated in October disappear by the end of the year and should be kept until April of the following year. Transitions emerge that germinate in October. You have to select your priorities, you can plan in the fall, but it's best not to instigate innovative change, but with all the facts at hand. Time should be spent to improve relationships, entertain, counsel, or inspire others.

Personal Month

The personal month in any one-year period provides the opportunity to complete projects, be charitable, and expand cultural activities. Personal ambitions will not be favored, nor will commercial aggression. Instead, it's time to inspire, counsel, and support others. Projects that started eight months ago flourish and will be completed or abandoned. Situations that require altruistic and open-mindedness arise. Visit the sick, the elderly, or the needy, bringing them a book, a tasty treat or a good ear. This is not the time to start anything! Group interactions, auditions, and public appearances enhance your reputation and attract rewards. Use this month to find outstanding or helpful people who have contacts or the ability to foster ambitions.

Personal Day

Wake up with a pleasant word and determination to solve all problems before sunset. Pass by the house of a friend in need and do something caring for him. Plan to share blessings, talents, and understanding. Use the day to tell the fanatic on the other street to grow up, and make sure that personal bias is not transparent. Detailed work may require effort too. It's best to put off the sewing, the iron, and the conversations with the accountant for a few days. It is a day to think about important issues and be generous with lovers, friends, and co-workers.

You will notice that there are giblets that need to be clarified and resolved. And the impulse to consolidate and to get out of the way everything that has been dragging is great. Make a personal commitment to be patient, forgiving, and well-meaning. Do not mix things up. Divide knowledge and let people who have lived and assimilated more than you enlighten them.

You will focus on people in cultural expansion and forgiving experiences. Listen to music, watch a play, or volunteer to donate blood. The only thing you can give that saves lives and restores itself in six hours is blood. Remember, to be creative; you first need to admire the art of others. It's time to get deep satisfaction by relating to your fellow humans and the universe.

Accept everything that happens today and is pleasant. Realize that there is an hour when it is necessary to give demonstrations of compassion, consideration, and tolerance. Certain sacrifices may be necessary. On this day, you may be blamed for someone else's mistake, or you can forgive and forget a slip. This day should be used to reflect, expand, or complete, and plan the changes of tomorrow. Above all, use the time to tie loose ends, and do not expect anything new to start.

Conclusion

Thank you for making it through to the end of Numerology: Decoding Your Destiny, let's hope it was informative and able to provide you with all of the tools you need to achieve your goals in life.

By gaining a deeper understanding of Numerology, you begin to understand the inner workings of your personality and the people around you. This makes life easier to navigate and gives you the power to work with what you have to succeed in all facets of life.

This type of knowledge and insight is certainly able to make you much more sensitive to what drives you and your personal needs. More importantly, it can also help you be in tune with the needs of others around you. As a result, you will be able to better communicate your needs and wants while connecting with others on a much deeper and meaningful level.

Please go refer back to this book as often as you need in order to clear up any questions you may have about the specifics of each number. Moreover, do keep this book handy since you will find yourself "reading" people all the time. As you gain more proficiency with each of the numbers in this book, you will develop a keen sense of the types of personalities people around your display.

If you have found this book useful and informative, do tell your friends, family, colleagues, and anyone who might be interested in this topic about it. They will surely find it to be as interesting as you have.